ABOUT THE AUTHORS

Dr Reg Saynor MSc, PhD, C. Chem, FRSC, FIMLS, and Member of the New York Academy of Sciences, is the Laboratory Director of the Cardiothoracic Unit, Northern General Hospital, Sheffield. He is a world authority on the 'Eskimo diet', having directed research into the beneficial effects of fish oil on preventing heart attacks for more than twenty years. He has given interviews, lectures and held seminars on the subject throughout Europe, the United States and Canada.

Dr Frank Ryan MB, ChB(Hons), FRCP is a teaching hospital consultant physician, gastro-enterologist and consultant medical advisor to the Nutrition Institute at the Northern General Hospital, Sheffield. He has had twenty years' experience dealing with the acute management of patients with heart attacks and a research interest in medicines. He is also the author of three novels *Sweet Summer, Tiger, Tiger* and *Goodbye Baby Blue*.

This book is intended only as an informative guide for those wishing to know more about reducing the odds of a heart attack. If you are at all worried about any aspect of your health, we strongly recommend that you consult your own doctor.

THE ESKIMO DIET COOKBOOK

Dr Reg Saynor
and Dr Frank Ryan

EBURY PRESS
London

For our patients

First published in 1990 by Ebury Press
an imprint of The Random Century Group
Random Century House
20 Vauxhall Bridge Road
London SW1V 2SA

British Library Cataloguing in Publication Data
Saynor, Reg
The eskimo diet cookbook.
1. Food: Low fat dishes. Recipes
I. Title. II. Ryan, Frank, 1944 –
641.5638
ISBN 0-85223-937-8

Phototypeset in Palatino by Textype Typesetters, Cambridge
Printed and bound in Great Britain by
Mackays of Chatham plc, Kent

Contents

Acknowledgments

We gratefully acknowledge the following for the help they have given us with the recipes: Barbara and Catherine Ryan, Margaret and Julie Saynor; Ebury Press; Mr John Moore and the Seafish Information Service; Pam Nelson and the Scottish Salmon Information Service; Val Treby, Denise Read, Cynthia Williams and Crookes Fisheries, Sheffield.

We are indebted to the authors and publishers who very kindly gave us permission to refer to and quote from the following copyright sources:

Coronary Heart Disease: Risks and Reasons by Professor A G Shaper, published by Current Medical Literature in association with Duncan, Flockhart & Co Ltd.

Coronary Heart Disease Prevention: Action in the UK 1984–1987, published by The Health Education Authority.

Guide to Healthy Eating, published by The Health Education Authority.

Provisional tables on the content of omega-3 fatty acids and other fat components of selected foods, published in *The Journal of the American Dietetic Association*, June 1986, *86*, pp 788–793.

Dietary omega-3 fatty acids and mortality in the MRFIT, presented to the Second International Congress on Preventative Cardiology, 1989, by Dr. Therese A Dolecek, Assistant Professor, Public Health Sciences, The Bowman Grey School of Medicine, Wake Forest University, North Carolina.

Introduction
What is the Eskimo Diet?

When, in March 1990, we published *The Eskimo Diet*, we had just one purpose: to give the ordinary man and woman the information he or she needs to cut down the risk of a heart attack to the bare minimum. Extraordinary interest was shown in the book from the start. The newspapers gave it a lot of coverage and the story was taken up by television and radio – it even attracted the humorous attentions of Clement Freud in his column in *The Times*. *The Eskimo Diet* was an instant best-seller. Why should a simple book written by two doctors provoke such a reaction?

The answer is that the information given was not the latest fad. Some people still seem to think that heart attacks are an act of fate which cannot be prevented. But you only need to consider a single fact to disprove this totally: as a result of deliberate changes in diet and lifestyle, in the United States the death rate from heart attacks in both men and women has been. more than halved over the last generation, while in the United Kingdom and much of western Europe it has hardly altered. The new information that has become available and which was the subject of *The Eskimo Diet* has shown how fish oil can greatly reduce the risk of a heart attack – indeed for eleven years Dr Saynor has been a world leader in the research into fish oil that has been responsible for the heart attack revolution. And now the message of *The Eskimo Diet* has been corroborated in the most remarkable way.

Within three weeks of the book's publication an article appeared in the *British Medical Journal* which examined for the first time ever the links between heart attacks and diet in women. This research had been conducted in thirty different hospitals throughout the north of Italy and confirmed exactly the advice we had given our readers.

On 23 March 1990 an international conference in Washington, attended by three hundred scientists from hospitals and laboratories worldwide, arrived at some very interesting and important conclusions. They considered the results of a study carried out by the US National Heart, Lung and Blood Institute (NHLBI), which, together with a report from the US Department of Agriculture scientists, showed that the typical American diet did not contain enough Omega-3 fatty acids (see p. 26), which are found in oily fish. In our book we had already reported this dietary deficiency, which is just as prevalent in the United Kingdom and Ireland as in many other Western countries. The conference also considered the results of Dr Dolecek's work, taken from the very important American MRFIT trial, which showed that a dramatic reduction in deaths from heart attack was achieved by eating oily fish. The report of the conference included this statement: 'New evidence with an extremely high level of statistical precision, from the NHLBI study, suggests that the daily intake of 0.5 to 1.0 grams of long chain n-3 fatty acids per day reduces the risk of cardiovascular death in middle-aged American men by about 40%.' Despite the technical language the message is clear; and our book had already recommended taking 800 mg (0.8 grams) of Omega-3 fatty acids per day. The report went on to say that 'some new data suggests that n-3 fatty acids may also decrease cancer mortality'. More will be said about cancer later.

In addition to confirming the role of oily fish and fish oil in preventing heart attacks, the conference made a further major statement: 'Based upon clear evidence of an essential role for Omega-3 fatty acids in human development and health, we recommend that *all diets for humans* should include Omega-3 fatty acids.' It went on to recommend that baby foods and intravenous and oral drips administered in hospital should include these essential ingredients.

Then, in April 1990, a National Institute of Health expert panel in the United States, with the support of thirty-eight national organizations including the American Medical Association and the American College of Physicians, made the very important recommendation that the entire population should be encouraged to reduce its consumption of saturated fat to precisely those limits given in our book, while increasing its consumption of oily fish, poultry without skin, vegetables, bread, cereals, peas and beans. Once again *The Eskimo Diet* had pointed the way.

So there it is. Not only has the medical profession provided powerful confirmation that our diet will help to prevent heart attacks – but it is also saying that this kind of diet is important for the general health of the whole population, from childhood to old age. This may seem extraordinary to people who up until now had thought fish was no more than a routine ingredient in the diet which you could take or leave as you fancied.

Although *The Eskimo Diet* contained a small number of recipes together with a week's sample menu, it did not aim to give comprehensive information on cookery. Many people who read it have asked for such a book, and now here it is.

This book is intended to be fully self-contained in its advice on menus and recipes, but for a more detailed explanation of heart attack and the scientific background to this story, readers should consult *The Eskimo Diet*. This new book will, however, still cover topics such as exactly how to change your diet, what kind of fish to eat, when and how to supplement your diet with fish oil or oil capsules, how to cut back on saturated fat painlessly, and how much fat you should eat – and you must continue to eat some fat or you will become ill. All of this can be achieved without making your diet boring; on the contrary, it can become all the more varied and exciting. Let's get away from the twin perils of fatalism and that dreary obsession with cholesterol. For our families sakes, let's increase our joy of living by putting a love of wholesome food back on the dining table.

1

Essential for Health

The Eskimo diet is not a panacea but it does offer a lot of benefits. Why? The answer lies with what we mean scientifically by an 'essential' fatty acid.

About 1930, in a search for ingredients that were vital for life, medical scientists tested the foods of animals. This was about the time when the major vitamins were discovered, but in addition they found that certain fatty acids, normally present in food, had to be included in a young animal's diet or it did not grow or develop normally. These 'essential' fatty acids were therefore very similar to vitamins: our bodies cannot manufacture them, yet they play very important roles in the running of our bodies.

What they had discovered was the 'essential' role of what are called Omega-6 fatty acids. They also looked at the Omega-3 fatty acids (see p. 26) but concluded that, since animals grew and their skins remained intact, these particular fatty acids were *not* 'essential'. In fact, because these early experiments were so basic, they were much too limited in their findings. Modern medical advances have enabled us to arrive at much more accurate definitions of what is 'essential', and we have no doubt at all that the Omega-3 fatty acids do play a vital and unique role in our bodies' chemistry. If we do not eat oily fish or take fish oil these essential fatty acids cannot do their work for us, and what we suffer from in consequence is a deficiency state very similar to the sort that would result from deficiency of an essential vitamin. It is not surprising, therefore, that this deficiency state should result in several different types of illnesses in different parts of our bodies, the most important of which is our tendency to suffer heart attacks. Now you will appreciate why the scientists in Washington came out with such clear recommendations for every single person to take fish or fish oil, and why the National Institute of Health in the United States recommended specifically that everybody needed to add oily fish to their diets.

Add to this the one most important statistic of all: the risk of a heart attack is so great, affecting one in three men and one in four women, that we have to consider we are *all* at risk. It is particularly important for mothers to get their children's diets right, since habits laid down in childhood are the proper foundation for a healthy diet for the rest of our lives. But there is everything to gain in adopting the Eskimo diet for anybody of any age, no matter if you already have artery disease – even if you have had a heart attack already.

The special and beneficial ingredients in fish oil are two unusual Omega-3 fatty acids. We cannot readily obtain them from any other dietary source and our bodies cannot manufacture them themselves: they are true 'essential' fatty acids. So there are two big questions to be answered. What role do they play in our normal body chemistry? And, even more important, what role do they play in disease?

The normal role of fish oil

This begins even before birth. There is clear evidence that DHA (see p. 26) plays a vital part in the development of the foetus. One of the important studies presented at the 1990 Washington conference demonstrated that if pregnant rats and monkeys failed to take in DHA, their offspring suffered from visual difficulties and learning problems later. The baby has to get its DHA from its mother's blood, so we strongly recommend the Eskimo diet to women in pregnancy. There is further evidence of an important link between the Omega-3 fatty acids and brain and central nervous system function, and this becomes particularly important as people get older. Several studies have shown that the elderly often suffer a deficiency of these very important fatty acids.

Most important of all, the Omega-3 fatty acids play a vital role in maintaining the health of our arteries. As Dr Saynor has shown during his years of intensive research, they keep the blood fats down, thereby reducing a major risk factor for heart attacks. They also lessen the tendency to form dangerous clots of blood within the narrowed coronary arteries which cause fatal heart attacks. They achieve this in two ways: by making the platelets in our blood less 'sticky' and lowering the level of the blood-clotting protein fibrinogen, which tends to be too high in Western countries, especially in smokers; and, more subtly, but very importantly, they have an effect on the delicate cells that line our arteries, making them less susceptible to injury and therefore to hardening of the arteries. A recent study using laboratory animals has even shown an ability to reverse pre-existing hardening of the arteries.

One of the major problems of growing older is that our blood vessels grow old with us, leading in many people to hypertension or high blood pressure. A number of important studies have shown that taking fish oil reduces our tendency to develop raised blood pressure. Fish oil also helps to prevent the adverse effect of certain blood pressure tablets on the fat levels in our blood. It may even be useful in treating patients suffering from raised blood pressure, but this is still being investigated.

A very interesting study by an Australian researcher showed that fish oil reduces the tendency of a diseased heart to develop serious electrical disturbances called arrhythmias. Other studies have already shown a potential role for fish oil in preventing such life-threatening arrhythmias after cardiac surgery.

One intriguing study of certain Japanese islanders has shown that they have unusally high levels of the fish oil Omega-3 fatty acids in their blood. These people live longer than any other Japanese.

A most important effect of these fatty acids is their tendency to reduce inflammation in our bodies. As a result of our Western diet, with its high proportion of Omega-6 fatty acids derived from vegetable and animal sources, we tend to form chemicals called eicosanoids. These substances promote inflammation in the joints and skin, and may perhaps even play a part in such serious diseases as bowel and breast cancer. This very important role is discussed below.

The benefits of fish oil in specific diseases

Heart attack

The most important benefit is the role that these fatty acids play in reducing our risk of suffering a heart attack. Dr Saynor conducted a seven-year study which showed an 80 per cent reduction in death rate from heart attack among patients taking fish oil regularly. (This is discussed in considerable detail in *The Eskimo Diet*.) Seven major medical studies worldwide have now looked at this, and in every case they have reported a major reduction in the death rate from heart atacks if people either eat oily fish or take a small dose of fish oil regularly. The dose of fish oil or the quantity of fish we recommend to our readers is based on the quantities which gave major benefit in these trials. It is important to realize that this benefit does not just apply to those who are fit and well, but also to those who have already suffered one or more heart attacks. It is never too late to begin the Eskimo diet.

Angina

An important trial, again performed by Dr Saynor, showed a significant reduction in angina among patients taking fish oil. This trial has since been confirmed by studies performed in Scandinavia. The desired results are probably achieved through a reduction of viscosity of the red blood cells, so that they can pass more easily through narrowed arteries.

Arthritis and rheumatism

After heart attacks, this is the most thoroughly researched aspect of the advantages of fish oil. Numerous studies have shown a significant reduction in pain, stiffness and inflammation in the joints of arthritis sufferers; it happens especially in the most serious form of the disease, rheumatoid arthritis, but also in the commonest form of all, osteoarthritis, which afflicts most people sooner or later in their lives. The way in which fish oil works here is almost certainly through the reduced levels of the 'inflammation' chemicals in our blood, as described on p. 13.

Psoriasis

This irritating and disfiguring skin condition affects one in every hundred of our population. Not only is it relatively resistant to many treatments, but the treatments themselves may sometimes have side-effects. There is evidence that sufferers may benefit from taking fish oil. Many studies have looked into this worldwide; most have shown some benefit, and some very marked benefit indeed. Not every sufferer makes a dramatic improvement, but overall there appears to be lessening of the redness and irritation in the skin of most who try it.

The action of fish oil in psoriasis may be due to incorporation of the Omega-3 fatty acids into the skin or to a lessening of inflammation. For example, fish oil reduces the amount of an inflammatory substance called leukotriene produced by the white blood cells under the skin.

The doses used in these psoriasis studies have often been higher than those we recommend, and such larger doses should only be taken under the advice and supervision of skin specialists. In general, for people who suffer from psoriasis there is little to lose in trying the modest doses we recommend and there might be a good deal to gain with regard not just to the skin condition but to the heart as well.

Cancer

The second commonest killer amongst the diseases we suffer from, cancer is probably the one which most frightens people. Recent research has shown that the incidence of some forms of cancer such as breast and bowel (colon) cancer is associated with a high consumption of fat in the diet. Taking Omega-3 fatty acids may reduce the incidence and development of breast, colon and prostate cancer. In *summarizing* the anti-cancer evidence in the *Journal of Nutrition* in the United States, Dr Aretemis Simopoulos wrote: 'In general, animal studies with various tumour models indicate that Omega-3 fatty acids have anti-tumour effects.' In other words, the fatty acids in fish oil tend to fight against cancer. This evidence that fish oil is of benefit against cancer is, however, very new, and has only been confirmed to date in animals. This means that it has a long way to go before it would be considered to be of proven benefit in human disease. The preliminary evidence suggests that the effects are achieved once again through a reduction of the 'inflammation' chemicals in the body.

Malaria

In countries with a tropical or sub-tropical climate, one of the major health hazards is malaria. Research in the United States suggests that the Omega-3 fatty acids may have a useful role in the prevention and treatment of human malaria.

Other diseases

The potential benefit of fish oil in various other conditions is currently being investigated. These include bowel ailments such as ulcerative colitis and Crohn's disease, but the work is at much too early a stage to give a proper assessment.

2

The Importance of Diet

Remember how the nursery rhyme went?

> Jack Sprat could eat no fat,
> His wife could eat no lean...

Sadly, neither Jack nor his wife in fact got it right: it is as unhealthy to eat no fat as it is to eat too much of it. For example, the fat-soluble vitamins D, E, K and A are, as their name suggests, only found in the fat we eat – so that if you ate no fat at all your bones would eventually collapse, your skin would become covered in bruises, your eyesight would fail and you might even lose your sexual potency (if the three earlier mishaps had left you with any!)

Although this book is aimed at your inner health, not your outer girth, it is a marvellous bonus that the balanced diet we recommend will usually eliminate that weight gain of middle and later life and get your figure back to what it was when you were younger and trimmer. We must know exactly what we are eating when it comes to fat. So what is the right kind of fat, and just how much should we eat?

Argument and debate about the importance of cholesterol and saturated fat in our diet have raged for forty years – and still rage today. So let's start with the demon cholesterol.

What is cholesterol?

Cholesterol is found as a natural substance in all animal cells and blood. It is an essential element in our body chemistry – indeed we do not need to take it in our diets at all, because it is important enough for our bodies to produce it. In other words, it isn't a demon come to ravage mankind in the twentieth century. It is more a question of balance – and we have got the balance wrong.

Notwithstanding the conflicting opinions of the experts, an overall conclusion can be drawn from the mass of cholesterol research. In countries such as the UK, with a high average level of total blood cholesterol, the population runs a high risk of a heart attack.

Inherited raised blood cholesterol

Some people have what is called a familial tendency to high blood cholesterol – in other words it is an inherited problem. If several members of your family have suffered heart attacks (a history of sudden death is often very indicative), particularly in their forties, thirties or even younger, then you might be suffering from hereditary raised cholesterol. This affects about one person in five hundred and is referred to medically as hereditary or familial hypercholesterolaemia.

The risk of a heart attack for a patient with familial raised blood cholesterol is eight times the normal. If you suspect you may have inherited this problem, it is simple to arrange with your family doctor for the fat levels in your blood to be tested. A blood sample, taken when you are fasting, should include tests for cholesterol, HDL-cholesterol, triglyceride, and, hopefully, a calculation of the HDL/LDL-cholesterol ratio. Don't let the scientific terms put you off – they will all be explained a little later (see p. 19). The condition some-times responds to dietary advice, but some people may need to take a medication that lowers their cholesterol. Advice on this will be given by your family doctor – or in some cases by a hospital specialist if your doctor thinks it necessary.

Who should have their blood fats screened?

We make no apology for what may appear a controversial statement: everybody in the population should be screened. Yes, this does include children, especially if there is a strong family history of coronary heart disease or known high risk of atheroma (fatty deposits in the arteries, which eventually block them). In families with hereditary high blood fats, even very young children may be affected and must be screened. All the big atheroma trials have indicated that it starts early in childhood, so the sooner we spot high-risk people and do something about it the better. Screening is possible on the Health Service or privately and it only involves a simple blood test.

What are HDL-cholesterol and LDL-cholesterol?

Cholesterol is manufactured mainly in our livers – and, as already noted, it is a vital chemical for our body cells. How does it get to all of these cells, since it is completely insoluble in water?

The answer is that it has to be kept in solution by some tricky chemistry inside our vital organs. The body produces particles made up of protein and fat that act as transporters for cholesterol in our blood – in other words it is carried about dissolved in tiny little droplets. These transporting particles are recognized by receiving stations on the walls of our cells, where the cholesterol is accepted. The process continues in a businesslike manner – until something goes wrong.

The main particle involved in ferrying cholesterol is low density lipoprotein or LDL. It arrives at the liver, picks up its cargo of cholesterol, and transports it into the blood en route for the cells throughout the body. Problems arise if there are too few sites in the tissues for the LDL to dock at, and so it starts to dump its load in all sorts of areas where this really shouldn't happen. This is why doctors are more interested these days in a high level of LDL-cholesterol than in a high level of whole-blood cholesterol.

One of these unwelcome dumping grounds is the lining of the coronary arteries. The frightening thing for us in the Western world is that this excessive dumping of fat, or atheroma, starts so early in life; the very first evidence of the process can be seen in the coronary arteries of young children. Pathologists who performed post-mortems on young American soldiers killed in the Korean War were astonished to find such advanced atheroma in men who were barely out of their teens.

Obviously, we in the Western world eat too much

cholesterol and this adds to the body's problems of over-loading. But the way to deal with this situation is not an obsessive preoccupation with every milligram of cholest-erol in our diet. Indeed the problem has more to do with saturated fat than with cholesterol, and this will be ex-plained a little later (see p. 23).

There is an ancient theory called the Doctrine of Agues, which says that wherever you find a malady, a benevolent providence will have also provided the cure. All you have to do is look for it. In the human body, providence has provided a counter to excess cholesterol in another small particle called high-density lipoprotein, or HDL. This, too, is produced in the liver. As the HDL circulates, its main function is to scavenge excess tissue cholesterol, which it picks up and returns to the liver for disposal.

An eminent doctor in the United States, William Castelli, reported that a man in his early thirties had died in his sleep; the results of a post-mortem examination showed that his arteries were hopelessly furred up with cholesterol-laden atheroma. The baffling thing was that this unfortun-ate man did not have high blood cholesterol. Intrigued, Dr Castelli investigated more closely. He discovered that the young man's ability to clear cholesterol from the blood was very poor. So although his total cholesterol was normal, he could not ferry it properly back from the tissues to the liver. He had a low blood HDL. Subsequent research has confirmed this finding. If you have a low HDL-cholesterol you are at greater risk of a heart attack.

Your total cholesterol/HDL-cholesterol ratio

A quick way to find out if you have a high risk factor for heart attacks is, once you have had your blood fats tested, to divide your HDL-cholesterol count into your total cholesterol count. If the figure you get is around 4.95, you have an average risk. If the figure is higher than this your risk increases, and if it is lower the risk is less than average. Adding oily fish or pure fish oil to your diet can increase your level of protective HDL-cholesterol. Your body does this by modifying the chemistry of another fat called triglyceride.

What are triglycerides?

Examples are the white 'lardy' fat you see on meat, on the top of a pint of fresh full-cream milk, or floating in the pan as all-too-delicious melting butter! This is the kind of fat that contains those well-known risk factors referred to as *saturates* and *unsaturates*, which will be explained below.

Triglycerides are made up of two main ingredients. The first of these is called glycerol, and a single molecule of glycerol has the chemical shape of a three-pronged gardening fork. The second ingredient, called fatty acids, comes in three parcels, each of which bonds itself to one prong of the glycerol molecule. This new chemical, made from the joining of three molecules of fatty acid on to one molecule of glycerol, is called a triglyceride.

As fats, triglycerides are one of the body's most important energy sources. Gram for gram, they are more energy-rich than sugar or carbohydrate. They can be taken directly from the food we eat or can be manufactured in the liver, where they are used to store energy for when we make our muscles work hard and require a large supply of triglycerides.

Why is triglyceride so important in preventing heart attacks? When Hugh Sinclair, the great pioneer of fish oil, examined Eskimos in their natural environment he found that, although they were virtually free of heart attacks, their blood cholesterol level was quite close to that in the UK. What was different was the level of their triglyceride. In spite of their very high intake of animal fat, the level of their triglyceride was only a quarter of the average level in the UK.

Here in the Western world, if we eat a lot of fat we can expect high triglyceride levels in our blood. The early researchers such as Sinclair expected high levels in Eskimos and were astonished to find that the triglyceride levels were so very low in their blood. At the time they were utterly baffled. We believe we now know the explanation: there are fatty acids unique to fish which actually lower triglyceride in our blood. We shall return to this topic shortly (see p. 26).

General advice about being overweight

What we mean when we talk about unwanted body fat, is stored triglyceride. When we eat this kind of fat, it is broken down in the gut by digestive enzymes, only to be reassembled within the body and transported by another of the protein carrier molecules, VLDL (very low-density lipoprotein), to our fat stores, where it usually makes us unhappy. In women, fat is preferentially distributed to the bust, bottom, abdomen and thighs. In men it shows a more even body distribution, although they too show a marked tendency to accumulate it in the big elastic space between the chest and the pelvis.

The more we eat of foods containing triglyceride, the more fat is stored: it is, more or less, a simple equation. Fat is energy stored. When we exercise, whether it be a gentle walk or a tough game of football or hockey, our muscles need a supply of energy. The body nips off a bit of fat from our reserves and chops down the molecule so that the fatty acids (now called free fatty acids) are released, to be burnt up in the muscle cells. If we do no more exercise than walking to the television set or the biscuit box, then we won't burn up a great deal of fat. Unfortunately, there is a vicious circle in which we continue to eat food at a rate laid down in our more energetic youth, fat builds up in those bulgy bits of us, we get slower and feel less like exercising, and so on.

Being fat does not itself lead directly to a heart attack, although it is linked closely with several factors that do increase the risk, such as hypertension, raised blood triglyceride levels, raised blood cholesterol levels and reduced physical activity. If these other factors are not present, then, surprisingly, obesity in itself is not a risk factor. Even more surprising, perhaps, is the fact that those people who can binge on food to their heart's desire and still remain reed-slim are not immune to heart attacks.

How does this relate to heart attacks?

Our researches have shown that in people with a higher than normal triglyceride level, tested while they are fasting, the HDL is usually lower than it should be. If we reduce our blood triglyceride by cutting down on saturated fat in our food, the HDL in our blood will probably increase. Here we encounter another of those wonderful properties of fish oil. Although it is a fatty acid, it has powerful protective effects on the level of triglyceride in our blood.

Alcohol and sugar

Sadly, alcohol does have the effect of raising fat levels in the blood; and so, if indulged to excess, does sugar. But don't get depressed – it's all a matter of balance and common sense. We would not claim conclusive proof that a glass of wine or beer a day actually helps – although the incidence of coronary heart disease is a lot lower in France than in the UK – but, taken in moderate quantities, alcohol increases our enjoyment of life and certainly does not cause the vast majority of the population any harm. Nor do we say you cannot have any butter, cheese, meat, milk or sugar. What we are saying is that in the UK we consume *too much* of these products.

Oral contraceptives

Some pills increase cholesterol and triglyceride, while others are actually beneficial, increasing HDL-cholesterol. In general it appears to be the oestrogen in the pill which is beneficial to women, and the newer pills have been formulated with this, amongst many other factors, in mind.

Exercise

Other activities to increase the protective levels of HDL in our blood include exercise, weight reduction, and in general a healthier, fitter lifestyle.

What are fatty acids?

Let's talk just a little about another of those components that make up the complete molecule of triglyceride – the fatty acids.

These are the 'polywhatsits' that give the Sunday newspapers such fun in their headline material. They are the basic components of all fats and oils – indeed they are the building blocks from which fats and oils are made. There are three common types of fatty acids, saturated, polyunsaturated and monounsaturated. The physical differences between these three types may appear to be trivial, but in the internal chemistry of our bodies such differences are devastatingly vital.

Saturated fats

A fatty acid is basically like an open necklace of carbon atoms (like little black pearls) with an acid chemical group at one end of it. If the chemical links between the carbon pearls are single, the fat is saturated.

Unsaturated fats

If any of the links are double, the fat is unsaturated. One double link (called a chemical double bond) and it's a *monounsaturate*. Two or more along the necklace (chemical chain) and it's a *polyunsaturated* fatty acid.

Hydrogenated fats

Saturated is a chemical term referring to whether or not you can attach any more hydrogen atoms. If there are no double links left, you cannot. If there are, you can break a double link into a single, releasing two more chemical positions to which hydrogen atoms can be attached. This also explains another confusing term, *hydrogenated*, which is frequently found in nutritional labels on food. For example, a hydrogenated vegetable oil may have started out life as a polyunsaturate, but hydrogenation means the double links have been broken and hydrogen added. The vegetable oil is therefore no longer a polyunsaturate but a saturate.

Examples of saturated and unsaturated fats

One or two examples will put you in the picture. Lard or dripping is composed mainly of saturated fatty acids (the ones that are bad for us) and this results in a hard fat. Olive oil is composed mainly of monounsaturated fatty acids and is quite fluid in warm temperatures, but can become thick and less runny when cold. Corn and vegetable oils are mostly polyunsaturated fatty acids and remain fluid at quite low temperatures.

Saturated fats are nothing other than fats that contain mostly saturated fatty acids, whether in their native chemical state or making up part of triglyceride molecules. For many years we have indulged ourselves in large quantities of saturated fats in the form of chips, Sunday joints and roast potatoes cooked in the meat dripping, not to mention the tasty traditional bacon, eggs, fried bread and, in Northern England, Scotland and Ireland, black and white puddings, which are enormously high in saturated fat. If you knew how much saturated fat beef and pork sausages contained, you would be very surprised!

Why saturated fat is bad for modern man

This story can be used to sum up the effects and functions of blood fats. It is set in a forest in Ancient Britain. A young man, entirely naked except for a coat of blue woad (or was it the British climate?), was squatting and eating his lunch while looking furtively over one shoulder and then the other. No doubt he was afraid of being attacked by a sabre-toothed tiger or some such hungry animal. Suddenly there was a roar behind him and immediately his heart started to race as the adrenalin flowed. At the same time, triglyceride was released from his fat stores and converted into free fatty acids to supply energy for his escape. He ran and ran until he could no longer hear his enemy behind him; in so doing he used up the released triglyceride and his heart slowed down as the adrenalin supply decreased. As well as increasing the heart rate, adrenalin also increases blood triglyceride levels.

His modern counterpart is likely to be sitting in his office when the telephone rings. His boss exclaims, 'What the hell happened to that report I asked for – do something about it!' Immediately our poor friend's adrenalin flows, his heart rate goes up and his triglyceride level is raised. But does he immediately spring into all-out exercise to use up this potential energy? He is far more likely to tense up over his desk, light a cigarette and stew in his high adrenalin, persistently raised triglyceride, ongoing high heart rate and raised blood pressure.

To give another example, closer to our own times, people will often point to one of their elderly relatives and say: 'But look at my grandmother! She's eaten dripping and cream all her life and she's ninety-two.' This may well be true. But the grandmother in question usually worked very hard physically in the home, did not have a car to ferry her to work or to the shops, never sat back for hours watching television, did not live and work in a centrally heated environment, and so on. There is a balance between fat consumed and energy output, and today we exercise a great deal less than our parents and grandparents.

So what is special about fish?

Imagine what would happen if fish, living in cold waters, were fed the saturated fats we tend to eat! The cold would make the fats in their blood congeal, and the blood flow would slow down until the fish became as stiff as a board. Clearly they must eat polyunsaturates of a special kind which remain fluid at cold temperatures.

Fish contain special fats because they themselves eat polyunsaturated fats of a very special type. These fats have a double link between the third and fourth carbon pearl, the so-called '3' position, and so they are called n-3 (or Omega-3) fatty acids.

The vital Omega-3 fatty acids in fish oil

The vital ingredients in fish oil, EPA and DHA (which are much easier to remember than what they stand for, the tongue-twisting eicosahexaenoic acid and docosahexaenoic acid), are two of those Omega-3 polyunsaturated fatty acids. As explained earlier, they are very special ones, known as 'essential' fatty acids, which means our bodies cannot manufacture them on their own. The only way we can get them is through our diet, and they are only found in oily fish or in special preparations of fish oil.

3
Getting Our Dietary Balance Right

There is a great deal of truth in the saying, we are what we eat. Now we understand that eating oily fish or taking a small regular intake of fish oil has dramatically beneficial effects on our blood chemistry, particularly on our blood fats and the mechanisms that lead to clotting in our arteries. These effects are so impressive that, taken with the dramatic reduction in our consumption of oily fish in the Western world during the latter part of the twentieth century, it is now possible to outline a very simple and likely hypothesis.

The cholesterol story, clearly of great importance in itself, has always puzzled doctors because they were well aware that it was an incomplete story. Given the reductions in cholesterol that can be achieved just by cutting down the amount of saturated fat in the diet, the mortality from heart attacks remained very high. It may well be possible that with fanatical adherence to an almost unpalatable diet, coupled with powerful drugs, the blood cholesterol can be lowered to hitherto unknown levels – but common sense would tell us that this not a natural approach to diet. Foods such as meat, eggs, butter and cheese are natural ones, eaten by human beings since long before the modern epidemic of heart attacks. Any advice given about their consumption can only be a question of *how much* we eat; it could not possibly be natural to rule them out altogether. While this type of *treatment* may be the only way to deal with the rare and serious hereditary disorders of blood fats, it is not practicable for the majority of the population. Yet that same majority must take the risk of heart attack very seriously indeed.

Our strategy aims at moderation in both diet and lifestyle. We all need a reasonable amount of fat in our diets, since without it we would suffer the serious consequences of deficiency of the fat-soluble vitamins such as A and D. We therefore suggest a common sense approach, based on a re-establishment of what we call the strategic balance.

In our opinion, the balance of the average Western diet has become seriously upset. It should not prove very difficult, and we hope might even prove pleasurable, to redress this. Clearly we need to put fish and fish oil right back into our kitchens and on to our dining tables.

Plan of the Eskimo diet

1. Eat oily fish at least twice a week, and supplement this with fish oil on the days you do not eat fish.

2. Although you must continue to eat some fat, keep the amount of saturated fat in your diet low, replacing it wherever possible with polyunsaturates and monounsaturates.

3. Eat more fibre and less sugar and salt.

4. Enjoy a drink, but go easy on the alcohol.

5. Above all, work your diet out so that it is varied and enjoyable – increase, not decrease, the happiness factor in your life.

Fish oil supplements as opposed to eating fish

We recommend a diet that stays as close to natural food as possible; therefore we suggest that you take your fish oil in the form of oily fish. This is not only pleasant and tasty, but has the added advantage of replacing meat as a main dish on the day you eat it, so reducing your intake of saturated fat into the bargain. The minimum recommended amount is only equivalent to 30 g (1 oz) of mackerel or 45 g (1½ oz) of salmon each day. If you take this amount daily, you do not need to take any fish oil as supplement.

For people who eat less oily fish, we would recommend that you supplement your diet with fish oil on the days you do not eat oily fish.

For people who eat little or no oily fish, our first recommendation must be that you try to develop a taste for this type of fish. There are so many oily fish on the market (see the comprehensive list on p. 31), and they make such varied and delicious meals, that you really are missing some great food experiences! A small number of people are genuinely allergic to fish and of course we would not recommend them to eat fish at all; but in his long medical experience, during which he has taken a special interest in food intolerance and allergy, Dr Ryan has found that most people with a so-called allergy are really expressing intolerances of or aversions to foods. If you are uncertain, discuss it with your doctor. If you wish to try something for the first time, eat a very small amount and test your reactions. Remember there are whole nations that live primarily on fish without any complications – indeed the evidence is that they do not suffer from many of the diseases we suffer from here in the Western World.

Some people will not be able or prepared to eat oily fish at all. Under these circumstances we recommend you to take all of your Omega-3 fatty acids as oil supplements. The subject of fish oil supplements was discussed very fully in *The Eskimo Diet*. Here is a very brief summary.

Which fish oil should I take?

When picking a fish oil you must take care that the manufacturer is established and reliable, and that the purity of the oil is guaranteed. We recommend Seven Seas Fish Oils since they are not only the major producer in the UK but also manufactured most of the oils used in the medical trials in the UK. They know exactly what is required, therefore, in a 'pure oil'. Other manufacturers' oils may be equally efficacious but you must check that they are not adulterated chemically. We do not at present recommend Omega-3 concentrates.

Once you have decided on the oil you wish to buy, work out your needs from knowing how much Omega-3 fatty acids it contains. We recommend a quantity which contains approximately 800 mg of Omega-3 fatty acids per day. You can calculate this by adding the amount of EPA and DHA given in the nutritional information on the packaging of the oil. Usually it will be between a teaspoon and a dessert-spoon. Capsules are a very good alternative for people who object to the taste of oil, but they tend to contain only small amounts and therefore taking the right dose may mean many capsules per day, at a higher cost than oil. Pure oil has the advantages of being cheap and very easy to swallow. Some fruit-flavoured oils are now available; these are very pleasant and easy to swallow, making them particularly good for children. Seven Seas Pulse Liquid Emulsion, for example, is banana-flavoured and you would need to take two teaspoons of this per day.

Can't I just take cod liver oil as my supplement?

Cod liver oil is quite similar to pure fish oil, but not identical. Fish oil is extracted from fish flesh (the meaty muscle of fish), whereas cod liver oil is made just from cod liver. This means that cod liver oil contains small doses of vitamins D and A, which in normal doses are beneficial but which, if taken in excess, could be unhealthy. Cod liver oil is otherwise an excellent source of fish oil and is reasonably cheap. Calculate how much you need on the basis of our recommended intake of 800 mg Omega-3 fatty acids per day. As an example, if you take Seven Seas Cod Liver Oil, two teaspoons daily would be sufficient; this quantity would not contain too much vitamin D and vitamin A.

I am a high risk case – shouldn't I take a larger dose of fish oil?

We accept that some readers may be at high risk and we would like to help them as much as possible. However, we don't recommend you to take a larger dose than the one stated except under strict medical supervision.

Will I experience any side-effects

Whenever a doctor prescribes a drug, she or he balances the potential for side-effects against the potential for benefit. Clearly the benefit usually greatly outweighs the risk of side-effects or the medicine would not be prescribed. *The Eskimo Diet* includes a comprehensive description of fish oil, its composition and a detailed discussion of its safety aspects. If for any reason you are worried, read the appropriate section in that book. In brief, if you are taking other blood-thinning drugs, such as anticoagulants or aspirin, if you suffer from a medical predisposition to excessive bleeding, or if you suffer from diabetes mellitus (whether you need insulin or just diet and tablets), we would advise you to take your oil by eating oily fish.

For the vast majority of the population, taking pure fish oil as a dietary supplement in the small doses we recommend is probably the safest 'medication' you could take. This is because it is not a medication at all in the usual sense, but the natural oil you would eat in a small portion of fresh fish. Millions take it in the form of cod liver oil every year throughout the world and have done so without serious effects for almost a century. Millions have also taken Pulse pure fish oil since it was first developed some ten years ago, and no toxic effects have been observed.

Which are the oily fish?

Different types of fish contain very different amounts of the protective oils. For instance cod, haddock and plaice, the favourites in the UK diet, are all poor providers. Fish can no more manufacture the essential EPA and DHA fatty acids than we can; they obtain their supplies from plankton, the microscopic organisms that float in the sea. Because of this, fish that have been bred in farms and fed soybean or other plant seeds or grains may be relatively poor suppliers of fish oil. As a general rule, fish netted from the sea or open rivers and lakes are the best. Since we criticized the feeds given to fish on salmon and trout farms in *The Eskimo Diet*, a number of fish farmers have approached us either to point out that their fish are healthy or to explain how they have altered their feeding habits to improve the fish. We have been assured in particular by the Scottish Salmon Growers' Association that their fish are properly fed. After examining their evidence we are delighted to reassure readers that Scottish salmon can indeed be highly recommended, and have therefore included it in many of our recipes.

Since there is now so much public concern about the adulteration of mass-produced foods, we feel the government should take a direct interest in farmed fish and set up standards for health and Omega-3 content. Salmon is particularly important since it makes delicious meals and is potentially one of the most beneficial fish, with high amounts of the Omega-3 oils.

The way we cook fish also has an effect on the oil content. Frying removes some of the oils. Grilling, baking, poaching or lightly boiling are all acceptable means of preserving the goodness. But prolonged boiling removes the oils from the flesh, and this can be a problem with canned tuna.

The following table is modified from an authoritative report entitled 'Provisional tables on the content of Omega-3 fatty acids and other fat components of selected sea-foods' by Hepburn, Exler and Weihrauch, published in the *Journal of the American Dietetic Association*. It lists the beneficial oils in most common and some less common fish. The fish are divided into three groups: highly beneficial, moderately beneficial and poorly beneficial. Within the sections, we have listed them according to the fatty acid content per 100 g (3½ oz).

Many readers will be familiar with buying and cooking fish. For those who are not, we suggest you first develop your skills with the more common highly beneficial varieties. As you gain experience, why not experiment somewhat and talk about some of the less common types of fish to your fishmonger or market trader.

The tables all assume fresh fish and uncooked weight.

Oil content of fish

Fish with a high fatty acid content (most beneficial)

Type of fish	Approximate n-3 fatty acid content as grams in 100 g (3½ oz) of fish
Mackerel	2.2
Spiny dogfish	2.0
Herring and sardines	1.7
Pilchards	1.7
Tuna (bluefin)	1.6
Trout (lake)	1.6
Sturgeon (Atlantic)	1.5
Salmon	1.4
Anchovies	1.4
Sprats	1.3
Bluefish	1.2
Mullet (unspecified)	1.1
Greenland halibut	0.9
Bass (striped)	0.8
Trout (rainbow)	0.6
Trout (Arctic char)	0.6
Trout (brook)	0.6
Mullet (striped)	0.6
Oysters	0.6
Carp	0.6
Squid (short-finned)	0.6
Tuna (skipjack)	0.5
Tuna (other unspecified)	0.5
Sturgeon (common)	0.4
Squid (Atlantic)	0.4
Bass (freshwater)	0.3
Squid (unspecified)	0.3

Fish with a medium fatty acid content (moderately beneficial)

Type of fish	Approximate n-3 fatty acid content as grams in 100 g (3½ oz) of fish
Hake (unspecified)	0.5
Mussels (blue)	0.5
Periwinkles	0.5
Shark	0.5
Catfish (brown bullhead)	0.5
Pollock	0.5
Hake (Pacific)	0.4
Sea bass	0.4
Shrimps	0.4
Crab	0.4
Perch (white)	0.4
Catfish (channel)	0.3
Perch (yellow)	0.3
Perch (ocean)	0.2
Hake (Atlantic)	less than 0.1

Fish with a poor fatty acid content (least beneficial)

Type of fish	Approximate n-3 fatty acid content as grams in 100 g (3½ oz) of fish
Pike (wall-eye)	0.3
Clams	0.3
Cod (Atlantic)	0.3
Cod (Pacific)	0.2
Plaice (European)	0.2
Scallops	0.2
Flounder	0.2
Lobster	0.2
Eel	0.2
Pike (northern)	0.1
Abalone	0.1
Haddock	0.1

From this comprehensive list it should be possible to devise many colourful and appetizing main meals. Try in time to extend your range of dishes and tastes, and remember that what at first seems strange and new may need several tries with different recipes before you really appreciate its attractiveness and flavour.

We would recommend that you aim for fish in the first two categories, in other words the high and medium fatty acid categories. However this does not mean that you should never eat the popular white fish in the low fatty acid category, such as cod, haddock and plaice. These are favourites with many people and make very attractive dishes, highly nutritious in other respects. They have a very important role as replacements on those days when your aim is to reduce your intake of saturated fat.

For instance, with reference to the menu section on p. 173, if you prefer a lovely meal of plaice on the day when we suggested perhaps a steak or vegetarian meal, eat plaice instead. Eating even the low fatty acid fish will give you a meal in which saturated fat is replaced by the more healthy polyunsaturated fish oils. But if you do, on those days simply take a fish oil supplement to ensure that you still get the full benefit of the Omega-3 fatty acids.

4

What to Eat on the Days You Don't Eat Fish

We are all aware that eating saturated fat and too much cholesterol is unhealthy for our hearts. In April 1990, Americans of all ages were urged to cut their risk of heart disease by reducing their fat intake. This was the first time ever that official health experts had issued such recommendations to the entire population and it excited enormous discussion and interest amongst American doctors and public alike. The guidelines had been drawn up by a National Institute of Health panel of experts and it had the support of 38 national organizations including the American Medical Association and the American College of Physicians. The recommendations were indeed precise and very comprehensive. We were delighted to see how closely these corresponded to the diet we had already recommended to readers of *The Eskimo Diet*. Attention to saturated fat (which is the best way of attending also to cholesterol) in our diet is the second half and equally important tenet of the Eskimo diet.

Essentially, what this panel recommended was that no more than 30 per cent of kilocalories should be obtained from all types of fat in our diet, less than 10 per cent of total kilocalories from saturated fat, and an average of less than 300 mg cholesterol per day. All of this should be worked into a diet which includes moderate consumption of oily fish, together with clearly understood quantities of lean meat, poultry without skin, fruit and vegetables, and a move towards low-fat dairy produce and skimmed milk.

Many will react with instant horror to what might sound

more like a mathematical exercise than an appetizing diet. Not a bit of it. The aim of this book is to show you how to achieve all of this without pain. Your family's diet should not only be healthy but also wholesome and enjoyable. You cannot be expected to count every kilocalorie you eat or every gram of saturated fat in the items you buy in the supermarket. Nor would we expect you to do so. The advice we give in this section should be interpreted as a general guide. It will help you just to know foods with a high saturated fat or high cholesterol. It will also enable you to interpret the tables of nutritional information you find on most foods these days.

It is most important that you do not go to extremes of either too much or too little. The recipes on p. 62 to 171 are intended as much as a guide to what you *can* eat as to what you should avoid. For example, some people think they should eat no fat at all – this is a disastrous policy since our fat-soluble vitamins and our 'essential' fatty acids are only to be found in fat. It is as bad for you to eat no fat as it is to eat too much.

Cutting down on saturated fat

Saturated fat usually arrives in the shopping basket in the form of animal and dairy produce, but it also has many more subtle forms. Cholesterol tends to come with saturated fat, but certain foods such as eggs, liver, kidneys and fish roe are very high in cholesterol while not so high in saturated fat. The following list contains some unexpected exceptions in categories which are otherwise good for you. Watch out for them. Everyone will find some items on the list which they are fond of: remember that you are not 'forbidden' to eat these, but you should try to reduce them to a minimum and allow yourself an occasional treat.

Foods containing saturated fat

Meat and meat products, such as beef, lamb, pork, suet, lard and dripping, are some of the chief sources. Very high saturated fats are found in brisket, corned beef, spare ribs, bacon, sausages and luncheon meats, and in fast foods such as hot dogs and hamburgers. High-cholesterol foods otherwise include liver, fish roes and – you might be amused to hear – caviar.

Dairy products, another major source of saturated fat, include full-cream and half-cream milk (but not skimmed), soft cheeses, butter, certain yogurts (not the low-fat varieties), certain ice creams (though you can get reduced-fat ice creams), custard made with full-cream milk, condensed milk, dried and evaporated milk. Also high in saturated fat are cheese spreads and dips.

Although the meats of chicken and turkey are excellent for being low in saturated fat, certain poultry, mainly duck and goose, are high in saturated fat. There is saturated fat in the skin of all poultry, including chicken and turkey.

Some vegetable oils, in particular coconut and palm oil, are surprisingly high in saturated fat (see p. 40) and should therefore be reduced considerably or avoided altogether.

Less obvious sources of saturated fat include cakes, doughnuts, pancakes, waffles, biscuits, chocolates (cocoa butter), cooking fats, hard margarines, sauces and puddings. Sauces in particular must be watched. Wherever possible, substitute natural yogurt or skimmed milk for cream, and the right kinds of vegetable oil, polyunsaturated margarine or low-fat spread for butter.

Remember that you can lose some of the benefit gained by a reduced intake of saturated fat if you use high-fat sauces or nibble high-fat snacks at lunchtime, or, most seductive of all, in that final snack before bedtime. A bonus from cutting down on saturated fat snacks is weight reduction, since fat contains more calories than any other food source. Because of the dangers of these regular snacks, it is well worth while setting your mind to alternative low-fat snacks and – more importantly still – making sure they are easily available for hungry mouths at the most dangerous times of day. Another great temptation, which we all suffer from, is rushing to find a quick bite and ruining a whole day's careful eating with a moment's temptation.

As a general rule of thumb, oils, fats, margarines and foods of vegetable origin will be rich in polyunsaturates and will usually contain no saturated fat. This is the basis of vegetarian diets, but vegetarian does not necessarily mean healthy, since dairy produce in particular, which tends to be a main ingredient of many vegetarian diets, contains very high proportions of saturated fats.

Another general rule is that cholesterol in our diet is usually bound up with saturated fat so that a diet low in saturated fat is also a low-cholesterol diet. There are a few exceptions to this – eggs, for instance, contain a lot of cholesterol in the yolk. Another food whose cholesterol content worried people for a time is shellfish – but in fact their initial concern may have been exaggerated. While this may still be controversial, the actual weight of shellfish per individual portion is usually small, so that there is no real worry about cholesterol content unless somebody is on a very strict low-cholesterol diet. This type of diet does not apply generally and would only be prescribed to those rare individuals with very high blood cholesterol levels which are resistant to changes in diet.

Foods containing monounsaturated fat

Oleic acid is the main example, and it derives its name from the oil in which it is commonly found, olive oil. Olive oil (and whole olives) is the best source, but others include avocados, peanuts, certain nut and seed oils and, perhaps surprisingly, meat fat, butter and eggs. On the continent, particularly in France and other Mediterranean countries where heart attacks are much less common than in the UK, it is the custom both to cook in olive oil and to place olive oil on the table for liberal consumption. While using olive oil in cooking is purely a question of practice and thinking about it in advance, its use in salads, for instance, is a question of taste. It would be a very good thing to encourage this taste. There is gathering evidence that olive oil does reduce the risk of a heart attack, and we might as well give it the benefit of the doubt.

Foods containing polyunsaturated fat

Polyunsaturates generally have a cholesterol-lowering effect and this is one reason why they are preferred to saturates. An additional very important reason is that, while they are fats and therefore contain important nutritional substances such as the fat-soluble vitamins, they are not thought to have any risk in connection with heart attacks. Therefore, they are seen as an ideal replacement for the saturated fat that needs to be reduced in the Eskimo diet. Fat should give you only about 30 per cent of your total calories, and of this less than 40 per cent should come from saturates.

It may help you to understand those figures in the nutritional information on food labels if we say that this means you take about 50 g (1¾ oz) of polyunsaturates and monounsaturates combined per day and a maximum of 30 g (1 oz) of saturates. Of course people don't go about all day calculating exact grams of fats, but a little time spent thinking about it or looking at labels in the supermarket will give you a surprising amount of information.

The EPA and DHA fatty acids in fish oil (collectively known as the Omega-3 or n-3 content) are examples of very special polyunsaturates. But those found in abundance in fresh vegetables (known as Omega-6 and non-fish oil type Omega-3 fatty acids) have special benefits of their own. These polyunsaturates are found in some vegetable oils, such as sunflower, soya, corn and grapeseed oil, in soft margarines made from these oils (look on the packaging and it will say 'high in polyunsaturates') and in nuts. The following table illustrates the main oils and fats and their average saturate contents. Nearly all of the rest of the oil or fat is in the form of monounsaturates and polyunsaturates. From a quick glance down this table you can check the cooking oil you use and choose a better one if necessary.

Oils

	Grams of saturates per 100g (3½ oz)
Coconut oil	85
Palm oil	49
Peanut/groundnut oil	19
Wheatgerm oil	19

Safflower oil	16
Soya oil	14
Sesame seed oil	14
Grapeseed oil	14
Blended cooking oil (poor quality)	14
Olive oil	13.4
Sunflower oil	13
Corn oil	11
Walnut oil	9
Blended cooking oil (good quality)	7

The next table shows you the fat breakdown of solid cooking fat. Notice that all of these contain more saturates than the vegetable oils commonly used in cooking, but once again there are huge variations between, say, solid sunflower oil fat and beef dripping. Once again, nearly all the remaining weight of the cooking fat is monounsaturate and polyunsaturate.

Solid Cooking Fats

	Grams of saturates per 100 g (3½ oz)
Dripping (solid beef fat)	59
Solid white cooking fat	47
Lard (pork fat)	38
Solid vegetable fat	26–50
Sunflower oil solid cooking fat	20

What about eggs?

Eggs are an excellent source of many nutrients. Unfortunately the yolk is high in cholesterol and because of this we advise you to limit your consumption to about three a week. One or two of these will probably come in the form of cooked food, but the remainder can be enjoyed as a boiled or poached egg (not fried) for breakfast.

Margarine versus butter

Should we eat butter or margarine? What about these newer butters which claim to be high in polyunsaturates? If you are the shopper in your family, how do you interpret the labels on these kinds of foods so you know what you are giving your family to eat? Remember that, as always, it is a question of quantity of saturated fat eaten rather than percentages. If you really like butter, full-cream milk, cheese, chocolate and so on, you can indulge yourself a little – but do it with knowledge of what you are doing and restrict the saturated fat to an average of less than 30 g (1 oz) a day. If you eat more one day, take less the next – so over, say, a week you keep it under control.

It is of course much easier to control quantity when the percentage of saturated fat is low, and this is the reason why polyunsaturated margarines have become so popular. We have examined the information provided on butter and margarine packets, and these are examples of what we have found.

Interpreting the nutritional information on butter and margarine

The butters and margarines we looked at were picked at random from our local supermarket, and we do not recommend these any more than other brands. What we do advise is that you insist that the food you buy does carry this kind of nutritional labelling, particularly when there is substantial fat present. Only by you, the customer, insisting will manufacturers and retailers get the message that you have an absolute right to know what you are eating.

Ordinary butter

Reading the label on ordinary butters tells you little, because they don't usually say what quantity or percentage of saturates they contain. On average the saturated composition of butter is about 60 per cent. The label will probably just tell you if it is salted or not.

Low-fat butters and margarines

Golden Churn

Nutritional composition per 100 g (3½ oz)

Energy (i.e. calories)	680 kcal (also expressed as 2830 kJ, i.e. kilo-Joules)
Protein	0.3 g
Carbohydrate (i.e. sugars, starches, etc.)	1.0 g
Fat	75 g
(of which saturates)	14 g
Salt	1.8 g

In other words, this brand of reduced-fat butter contains just 14 per cent of its weight as saturated fat in comparison with about 60 per cent in ordinary butter. We have to assume that the remainder of the fat content must be mainly polyunsaturates and possibly some monounsaturates. It would therefore be much easier to keep to less than 30 g (1 oz) a day of saturated fat if you ate this product.

Flora

Nutritional composition per 100 g (3½ oz)

Energy (calories)	740 kcal (3041 kJ)
Protein	0.3 g
Carbohydrate	1.4 g
Fat	80 g
(of which saturates)	14 g
Polyunsaturates	42 g

Notice first that the percentage of saturates in its total weight is the same as Golden Churn, at 14 per cent. But Flora, unlike Golden Churn, tells us the actual proportion of polyunsaturates, 42 per cent. The information on the pack does not, however, tell us what makes up the remainder of the fat (24 per cent of the total).

St Ivel Gold

Nutritional composition per 100 g (3½ oz)

Energy (calories)	390 kcal
Protein	6.5 g
Carbohydrate	2.0 g
Fat	39 g
(of which saturates)	10.5 g
Salt	1.3 g

This brand has a much lower calorie content than the previous two and the saturated fat percentage is slightly lower. In fact all three of these low-fat brands are considerably lower than ordinary butter in saturated fat. Choosing between them, or any other brand, is a matter of taste and concern for the other contents, such as calories and salt.

All three brands also give useful information on where the fat contents come from. They mention vegetable oils such as sunflower oil, hydrogenated vegetable oils (these mean saturated fat), skimmed milk, whey, lecithin (a chemical related to fat), flavourings, natural colours and vitamins.

The following table will give you a very clear idea of the average fat contents of different margarines and butter. It is again expressed as grams per 100 g (3½ oz), but the figures are very close to percentages of total weight. This table also includes a breakdown of the unsaturates into monounsaturates and polyunsaturates to give you some idea of what really does go into the composition of margarines and butter. Your guide is still, of course, the column headed 'saturates'.

Margarine, butter and low-fat spreads

	Grams per 100 g (3½ oz)		
	Saturates	Mono-unsaturates	Poly-unsaturates
Butter	49–60	27	2
Hard table margarine	35	32	4
Hard cooking margarine	31	32	12

Soft table margarine	22	39	15
Soya margarine	17	32	27
Sunflower margarines	14	24	42
Low-fat spreads	8	17	13

It is clear that you could eat five or six times the amount of low-fat spread as butter and only add the same amount of saturated fat to your intake. This principle also applies to hidden fats in cooking, or in bought foods such as confectionery and cakes. Keep an eye on the ingredients, which should be clearly stated on the packaging. Low-fat spreads are not suitable for cooking, but polyunsaturated margarines, such as sunflower margarines, often are.

A simple idea of how much saturated fat you or your family are already eating can be assessed by looking through your usual week's shopping at the supermarket. You'll only need to do it once to get a good general idea. Add up the saturated fat on the packages and cans, add to this an estimate from the meat, poultry and fish you buy, and make sure to include milk, cheese and any fast foods or items such as sweets and chocolates that are bought casually. Remember our guideline for daily total fat is about 80 g (3 oz) and for saturated fat about 30 g (1 oz).

The quality of margarines can vary a lot, depending on what type of oil they are prepared from. Sometimes the use of the term 'vegetable oil' can be misleading. If the manufacturer uses the term 'hydrogenated vegetable oil' or 'hydrolyzed vegetable oil' this means that an unsaturated vegetable oil has been converted into saturated fat by hydrogenation. The cheaper margarines and hard cooking fats may contain palm oil and animal fats, and this explains their much higher saturated fat content.

The harder a margarine or cooking fat is at room temperature, the higher the content of saturated fat. Vegetable margarines often need to be kept in the fridge, but don't let them get too hard since a softer spread goes further and this too helps to reduce the actual quantity eaten. Remember also that if you don't always win the war on saturated fat, you will still gain considerable benefit by eating more fish and by taking fish oil.

What sort of milk should I buy?

Have a look at the following list of saturated fat contents in a single bottle of different types of milk.

Milk

	Grams of saturates per 568 ml (1 pint)
Full-cream milk (gold top)	28
Ordinary dairy milk (silver top)	22
Semi-skimmed milk (red-striped top)	11
Skimmed milk (blue-hatched top)	1

The message is obvious. When you first change to skimmed milk, you miss the creamy taste and texture, but within a few weeks you will discover you prefer the taste of your breakfast cereal or tea unclogged by the overpowering richness of the cream content. Once again it is a question of quantity consumed over twenty-four hours; but taking skimmed milk allows you to drink as much as you like – and we are all for making life as easy as possible.

Condensed milk and evaporated milk contain a lot of fat, so avoid them whenever possible.

You will hear some people say that skimmed milk is nothing more than water or that it has had all of the goodness taken out of it. This is not true. Skimmed milk contains the same amount of calcium and milk protein as ordinary milk. But do not give skimmed milk to babies or very young children for whom milk is a major part of their daily diet. Under these circumstances the saturated fat is needed for a proper calorie intake and must not be left out.

But I love thick cream!

Most of us do. A tip for getting over the withdrawal symptoms is to use low-fat yogurt instead of cream whenever possible. Greek yogurt is particularly smooth and creamy textured. If you do use cream, use single rather than double. Beware of artificial creams, which often contain just as much saturated fat as real cream.

What about cheese?

Go for the ones with the least fat – see the general guide to fat intake in the table below. The joy of an occasional treat need not be denied.

Cheeses are natural foods, eaten since prehistoric times. If you like a particular cheese, or cheese in general, there is no reason why you shouldn't continue to do so. It is merely a question of how much you eat and how often. You need to take two factors into consideration: fat content (both total and saturated) and salt content.

A portion of cheese eaten with biscuits at the end of a meal can vary from about 30 g (1 oz) to more than about 125 g (4 oz). Under ordinary circumstances a small portion can easily be accommodated within the recommended daily total and saturated fat limits. 125 g (4 oz) of a cheese such as Cheddar, on the other hand, will equal two-thirds of your daily recommended intake of saturated fat. If you like large portions of cheese, try to develop a taste for a low-fat kind, or reduce the alternative sources of saturated fat in your diet, for example meat and other dairy produce.

When preparing sandwiches, you may find you can use less cheese if you buy ready-cut slices.

Here is a list of the total and saturated fat content of some common cheeses – but remember that these are for larger portions of cheese than most people eat. Note also that the difference between 'low-fat' and other kinds is huge, and that the 'medium-fat' category is much closer to 'high-fat' than to 'low-fat'.

Cheese	Total fat content (g) per 100 g (3½ oz)	Saturated fat content (g) per 100 g (3½ oz)
Low-fat		
Cottage		
creamed	4.8	2.8
1% fat	1	1
2% fat	2	1.5
Curd cheese	1	0

Cheese	Total fat content (g) per 100 g (3½ oz)	Saturated fat content (g) per 100 g (3½ oz)
Edam, low-fat (11%)	11.3	6.5
Quark skimmed milk	0.3	less than 0.3
Shape cottage	0.5	less than 0.5
Medium-fat		
Cheese spread	21	14
Delight	17	10
Feta	21.4	14
Mild goat's cheese (medium-fat, soft cheese)	18.1	12.6
Mozzarella		
part skimmed	17.5	10.5
full fat	20	12.7
Shape low-fat	16.5	10
Tendale	15	10
High-fat		
Brie	28	17.5
Camembert	24.5	14
Cheddar	33	22
Cheshire	31.5	21
Cream cheese	47	25
Edam	28	17.5
Emmental	28	17.5
Gouda	28	17.5
Gruyère	31.5	17.5
Kraft slices (Cheddar)	24	16
Parmesan	28	17.5
Roquefort	30.5	17.5
Stilton	40	26

It is relatively easy to estimate your consumption of fat from raw cheese, but the task is less easy when it comes to cheese-based dishes in ready-cooked foods or in restaurants. These can be a major source of saturated fat. The following table assumes average restaurant portions and that the cheese is a high-fat variety.

Type of Food	Total fat content (g)	Saturated fat content (g)
Cheese sandwich	25	15
Cheeseburger		
regular	13	6.7
quarter-pounder burger		
with cheese	26.4	14
Cheesecake	21	12
Cheese fondu	18	9
Cheese sauce	17	9
Cheese straws	18	8

Let's talk about meat

Meat, like dairy produce, is one of the highest sources of saturated fat in our diet. In the Third World, which may approximate to the difficult circumstances of our ancestors, very little meat is eaten. This is because meat is relatively expensive and vegetables are much cheaper and more plentiful. If we compare our consumption of meat today to that in nineteenth-century Britain, when heart attacks were very uncommon, it is much higher. We also eat less fish and bread.

We are not suggesting that you eat no meat. On the contrary, we think that you could eat it about twice a week as a main meal, which leaves room for some meat in sandwiches and snacks perhaps another twice a week. Here in the UK, butchers tend to cut meat across the muscle fibres (across the grain), which tends to keep the fat, which is trapped between muscle bundles. On the continent, particularly in countries such as France, which has a lower incidence of coronary heart disease, butchers tend to cut meat so as to remove any fat between the fibres. When you buy meat, pick the leanest cut you can find, and before cooking it cut off any fat. Do not add lard or dripping. Learn techniques for trimming off surplus fat from raw meat and scooping off liquid fat during cooking.

What's so special about chicken and turkey?

If you look at the meat in chicken, turkey or game, you will not find the thick white fat that you usually find between the muscle bundles and over the surface of red meat. Most of the fat in poultry is under the skin. There is a small amount in between the muscle of the meat, but this is very easily removed. Because of this, we encourage you to eat poultry, say, twice a week. But remember to remove the skin (and with it, therefore, most of the fat).

What's not so special about duck and goose?

Ironically, they are high in saturated fat and cholesterol, and so we need to treat them as high-fat meats.

Fat content of meat and fish

In general, about 40–50 per cent of the fat in meat is saturated. In chicken this is about 25 per cent, which is much the same level as in fish. Yes, fish does contain saturates too – but the relatively low levels are more than balanced by the polyunsaturates.

Will I become deficient in iron if I cut down on meat?

This is a very good question, since meat and liver are good sources of iron in the diet. To reduce saturated fat we have suggested that you only eat red meat in a main meal twice a week, so the possibility of not eating enough iron is a real one, especially for women before the menopause.

Our bodies only take in iron at a very low rate because in larger amounts it is toxic within the body. This means we need a good *steady* supply of iron in our diet. One way round this is to take a small dose of iron in the form of tablets such as Iron Jelloids. But be cautious. Many people don't tolerate iron tablets very well, and a normal healthy man or woman should only require a maximum of about 20 mg a day in his or her diet. In fact, we absorb only a tiny proportion of this, perhaps 1–2 mg, but we need the excess to 'make' the body take in this small natural requirement. We would recommend that you take your non-meat iron in the form of natural food rather than tablets – it is quite easy.

Iron is found in a wide variety of foods other than red meat or liver. Fish contains about a third of the iron level of red meat. Many vegetables contain good levels, for instance lentils by dry weight contain twice as much weight for weight as red meat, but it is not taken in quite as well by the body. Examples of excellent vegetable sources include lentils, kidney beans and pulses generally, baked beans, haricot beans and spinach. Make sure you include lots of these types of vegetable in your diet.

One excellent way of taking iron may well surprise you – fortified breakfast cereals. These have the additional advantage of containing other essential vitamins. Weetabix contains twice as much weight for weight as meat, All-bran about three times as much, Shredded Wheat about a third more and Bran Flakes almost seven times as much, all of these by dry weight of the cereal. Read your cereal packet and see how much iron it contains. It is quite possible that you can get all the iron you need in a day from your breakfast cereal alone.

More insidious foods that contain a lot of fat

These are often children's favourites – remember that here in the UK the first signs of atheroma in our arteries, the so-called fatty streaks, can be seen even in the arteries of our children. These hidden fats are to be found in crisps, chocolates, cakes, confectionery and biscuits.

Here again, we don't encourage fanaticism. The occasional little treat is what life is about – and you will find that crisps and cakes, for instance, are now available cooked with polyunsaturated oil, margarine or cooking fat. Try to reduce the amount you buy, and when you do buy, go for those with a lower saturated fat content.

General tips on cutting down fat in cooking

Some of the ideas in this section were inspired by the excellent booklet *Guide to Healthy Eating*, published by the

Health Education Authority. This is available free of charge from your local Health Education Unit, and we would like to thank the publishers for permission to borrow some of their ideas.

Often you can cut down saturated fat considerably simply by cooking differently. Take potatoes, for instance. If you eat them as a generous portion of chips you will consume approximately 240 calories containing 14 g of saturated fat (about half your daily allowance). With baked potato, you eat half the calories and virtually no saturated fat. But if you stuff the baked potato with sour cream and chives, you double the calories and ruin the whole plan by adding 24 g of saturated fat from the cream. On the other hand, if you use low-fat cottage cheese to stuff your potato, you reduce the additional calories by more than half and you reduce the saturated fat to negligible amounts. Here are some useful tips for keeping saturated fat down while still enjoying your food.

Avoid frying whenever you can. Grill, bake, poach or boil whenever possible. Another tip when frying is that you should only fry food with a high water content, say chips for example, twice or three times in the same oil. The process of frying 'hydrolyzes' the vegetable oil, converting the polyunsaturates to saturates.

Casseroling or stewing is an excellent alternative way to cook meat and it means you can buy cheaper cuts of meat – but remember always to *buy lean and remove as much fat as possible, even after cooking.* Place your cooked casserole in the fridge when cool. Once it has got quite cold the fat will have risen and solidified and you can break it off like ice on a pond. Then reheat your casserole when you want to eat it. Casseroles usually taste better when made in advance, anyway. After roasting, pour the meat juices from the roasting tin into a saucepan, add very cold water and put it into the fridge until the fat solidifies and floats on the surface. It is then relatively easy to spoon off the solid saturated fat and make your gravy from the rest. Another technique for separating off the fat is to add a trayful of ice cubes to the gravy, which serves the dual purpose of solidifying the fat and diluting the remains of fat in the gravy.

When *mashing potatoes*, avoid adding butter or margarine. You can add skimmed milk, which makes the potatoes very tasty and adds hardly any saturated fat at all.

When *preparing pâtés*, use skimmed milk or low-fat yogurt instead of butter, margarine or cream.

Chicken and poultry: casserole rather than roast, which allows you to take the skin off first. Remember that most of the saturated fat in chicken and poultry is just under the skin and comes away with it.

With *minced meat*, it is hard to tell how much fat there is in it. Even mince that looks quite red is usually quite fatty. Choose your own lean cut of meat and either mince it yourself or have it minced at the butcher's. There are several techniques for removing most of the fat. For example, just heat the mince in a pan, scoop it up with a draining spoon and put it on kitchen paper to drain off the fat. Then put the mince back into a clean pan and cook it in the normal way. Even simpler, heat up the mince in a pan and drain away the fat as it comes away from the meat.

Grill, steam, poach or bake fish. Don't deep fry it in batter – even in vegetable oil – since the batter absorbs a lot of the frying fat.

Use as little oil or fat as possible when cooking. Choose one that is low in saturates and high in monounsaturates and polyunsaturates (see tables on p. 40 and 41). Sunflower, soya and corn oils are best, followed by olive oil. Place some olive oil on the table and encourage the family to develop a taste for it, especially on salads.

Avoid lard, coconut oil, palm oil, hard margarine, butter and ghee. Mixed vegetable oils can be very confusing and contain a lot more saturated fat than pure vegetable oil, so it is best to leave them well alone.

When *stir-frying* it is best to use a steep-sided, round-bottomed pan like a wok. These allow you to fry using a small amount of oil.

If you must fry, use a non-stick pan and you might not have to add any fat or oil at all.

Convenience and fast foods

Convenience foods are not necessarily junk foods. Many are first class – for instance frozen peas, tinned beans and frozen fish. The problem arises with products such as pies, burgers, hot dogs, sausages, biscuits, chocolates, crisps and so on. It may be very difficult to know what is in a product such as pre-packed pizza unless it is stated on the packaging.

Take a few examples: In a food very popular with children, such as pizza, the saturated fat content will depend on what fat is used in baking the bread base, which cheeses are put on top and the quantity and type of meat, if any, that is included in the topping. It should be possible to make your own pizzas with relatively low-fat ingredients, but if you eat out or buy a pizza ready-made, then you must consider the fat content as part of your planned intake.

The Massachusetts Medical Society Committee on Nutrition looked into the amount of junk food eaten in the United States, and their results were published in the *New England Journal* in September 1989: 'Every second, an estimated two hundred people in the United States order one or more hamburgers.' On a typical day, one in five Americans eat at a fast food restaurant, of which there were 140,000 in 1980. Britain appears to be following the American lead. With hamburgers and hot dogs, as with sausages, assessing how much saturated fat you are eating is difficult but not impossible (see list below). Official definitions of meat content may be very misleading – for instance in sausages a declaration of, say, 60 per cent meat could result in a great deal of saturated fat being retained, because meat is defined as a minimum of 50 per cent lean. In pies there is extra fat in the pastry. If you eat a lot in this type of restaurant, try changing to baked potatoes, salads and leaner meats or non-battered fish. Restaurants are, after all, acutely sensitive to what the public wants. It's up to us, the customers, to call the tune.

A general tip is to be suspicious of all so-called junk food. Inspect the labels for percentages of unsaturated fat and assume that the rest must be saturated. Many of the fast food restaurants in the UK are now following the American lead and declaring the fat content of their meals. This will certainly help you in working out your daily intake and should therefore be encouraged.

The following list is not comprehensive but includes

many fast and convenience foods. Where we give the amount of fat for an item of food, rather than 100 g (3½ oz), we assume an average-sized portion. We are grateful to Wimpy and McDonalds for the information given on their meals.

Fat content of fast and convenience foods

Type of Food	Total fat (g) per item	Saturated fat (g) per item
Traditional UK foods		
Sausage roll	20 per 60 g roll	assume 10
Steak and kidney pie	42 per 200 g pie	assume 21
Pork pie	38 per 140 g pie	assume 19
Fruit pie with pastry	15.5	4.3
Fried fish in batter	20 for large fish	depends on cooking oil
Chips, fried	22 for chip-shop portion	depends on cooking oil
Black pudding	22 per 100 g	assume 50 per cent saturate
Mayonnaise	78.9 per 100 g	varies with oil
Yorkshire pudding	10.1	varies with cooking fat
Fried pork sausage	14.7	assume 7.3
Frankfurter (large)	12.5	assume 6.3
Toffee	17.2 per 100 g	assume 7 g
Chocolate	32 per 100 g	assume 18 g
Fast food restaurants		
Wimpy		
Hamburger	9.6	assume 4.8
Cheeseburger	13	assume 6.7
King-size Wimpy	20.6	assume 10.4
Quarter-pounder	30	assume 15
Half-pounder	51.4	assume 25.7
Bacon and egg in bun	23.4	assume 11.7
Milk shake	6.6	assume 6.4

table continued overleaf

Fat content of fast and convenience foods
(continued from p. 55)

Type of Food	Total fat (g) per item	Saturated fat (g) per item
McDonalds		
Hamburger	9.9	5.0
Cheeseburger	13.6	6.7
Quarter-pounder	19.3	9.1
Quarter-pounder + cheese	26.4	14
Fried fish	24.6	5.3
French fries (regular portion)	14.5	7.9
Chicken nuggets	16.4 per six	4.4 per six
Apple pie	15.4	4.3
Plain doughnut	16.3	7.6
Choc doughnut	19.5	10.2
Milk shake	6.1	4.3

The importance of fibre

Fibre is the background skeletal structure of many plants, such as cereals (wheat, oats, corn, etc.), most vegetables and most fruits. It also has another great advantage: none of the fibre in a food is lost through cooking.

The modern interest in fibre came from the realization that people in the Third World, who do not suffer from 'Western diseases', eat much more fibre in their diets than us. We eat about 20 g (¾ oz) a day whereas in Africa, for instance, they eat more than 100 g (3½ oz) a day. This was believed an important contribution to the fact that on their native diet Africans do not suffer from irritable bowel syndrome, constipation, diverticular disease and possibly even large bowel cancer. They also have a lower incidence of dental decay and gallstones. More fibre in the diet may improve the control of diabetes, and can greatly help to reduce weight because food high in fibre tends to be filling in relatively small amounts. Increasing the amounts of fibre in your diet may also have additional benefits in preventing coronary heart disease.

Soluble and insoluble fibre

There are two types of fibre: water-soluble and water-insoluble. Most of what we recognize as high-fibre food contains water-insoluble fibre, for instance wheat bran. This is the type that helps prevent or control bowel complaints. Most of the fibre in oats and beans is water-soluble and this is the type that appears to be most promising in the control of heart disease. It is best taken in the form of oat bran or oatmeal, for instance in breakfast cereal or in bread or baking.

Fibre is obtained in meals that include beans, wholemeal bread, oatmeal bread and cakes, and wholemeal pasta. Adults should try to eat at least 30 g (1 oz) of fibre a day (about the same amount as saturated fat).

How to eat more fibre

Eat plenty of bread, preferably in thick slices. Choose wholemeal rather than white. Chapatis, hard dough and pitta bread are very good, provided they are made from wholemeal flour.

Use wholemeal flour instead of white flour for baking.

Choose the right breakfast cereal. Many of these are high in fibre as well as vitamins and iron.

Deliberately increase the amount of peas, beans and lentils you eat. Beans in particular may make the basis of a meal themselves. Canned beans are just as good.

Eat more potatoes, which are an excellent source of energy in the form of carbohydrate. Most of the fibre is, however, in the skin, so try baking them in their jackets. Sweet potatoes and yams are equally good sources of energy and fibre.

Brown rice is better than white. It may take a bit longer to cook, but doesn't stick to the same extent and tastes nicer.

Make a policy of putting out *unsalted* nuts and dried fruit and take these as mini-snacks instead of biscuits or chocolates. Be careful, however, about eating too many if you are trying to lose weight, since they contain quite a few calories.

Try to eat fruit and a good range of vegetables at least

once a day. They not only contain a lot of fibre and are filling without containing too many calories, but they also contain very important vitamins.

How to read the nutritional content of food

Most supermarket foods now give nutritional information, and it is easily understood if you read the contents carefully. Somewhere on the packet, can or bottle you will find a list. For example, on a 450 g (1 lb) can of Heinz baked beans the contents read:

Amount per 100 g (3½ oz) [note: a serving is about 225 g/8 oz]	
Fat	0.3 g
(of which saturates)	0.1 g
Protein	5.0 g
Carbohydrate	13.1 g
(of which sugars)	6.0 g
Energy	306 kJ/72 kcal
Sodium	0.5 g
Dietary fibre	7.3 g

Interpreting this should prove easy. There are 72 calories in every 100 g (3½ oz), or 162 calories per 225 g (8 oz) serving. Very little is fat, and only 0.1 g is saturated fat. Most of the calories clearly come from carbohydrate, of which roughly half is sugar. There is a great deal of fibre present, but whether soluble or insoluble is unspecified.

Carbohydrates

Once upon a time, slimming diets were low in carbohydrate and tended to include quite a lot of fat early in the day. Remember the old slogan: 'Eat fat to lose weight'? With better understanding we now prize complex carbohydrates as excellent sources of energy and vitamins, and they form an integral part of a balanced healthy diet.

The two commonest sources of complex carbohydrates are bread and potatoes. Apart from the calorie considerations, these are both very healthy and nutritious components of our diet and we use plenty of them in our recipes. With bread, choose a high-fibre type such as wholemeal or oatmeal. With potatoes, avoid roasting them and keep chips to once or twice a week, following tips already given about cooking them. Boiled potatoes are good, provided you don't melt butter over them. Baked are even better and very quick these days in a microwave cooker. Try to eat the skin too: it is an excellent source of fibre. Flavour your jacket potatoes with low-fat cottage cheese or natural yogurt with chives.

Salt

Let's not get too carried away about salt. The majority of the population can cope very well with the 10 g or so we eat in our daily diet. But a minority cannot. These are people with a tendency to raised blood pressure, people with certain types of heart disease, liver disease and kidney disease. If you have raised blood pressure you will undoubtedly be under the care of your doctor, who will advise you on salt intake. People who already suffer from heart disease will also take sensible precautions about salt. But this does not mean taking no salt at all. It is vital, and with no salt in our diet we would become very ill indeed. Most of us need only 1 g a day for our body's needs; we eat the other 9 g because we have developed a taste for it. Salt's only connection with heart attacks is its link with high blood pressure.

Most of the salt we eat is put into our food at the processing, manufacturing and cooking stages: 75 per cent of our intake gets into our food in this way. Some comes in ready-bought food, more is added during cooking and only about 15–25 per cent is sprinkled on our food before eating it. If you would like some general tips about salt intake, you will find some overleaf that might help:

Use less salt in cooking.

Use less in flavouring, or try other flavours such as lemon juice, herbs, spices, pepper and mustard. Salt substitutes, obtained from the chemists, contain less real salt than ordinary table salt but most still contain some salt. These are not necessary at all for the average person's diet. Sea salt has other minerals in it but is no better than table salt in its general salt content.

Cut down on salty snacks such as crisps and salted nuts.

If you buy tinned vegetables, buy the ones marked 'no added salt'.

Cut down on ready-salted meats and fish such as bacon, gammon, salt beef and salt mackerel.

Use fewer canned and packet soups. A single serving can contain 1–3 g of salt. Make your own soups instead.

Putting all the dietary advice into practice

We have given a lot of dietary advice in this chapter. You should now aim at bringing the two broad aspects of the Eskimo diet together, by increasing your consumption of oily fish and reducing your consumption of saturated fat. You will find it quite easy to incorporate the other aspects, such as increasing your consumption of fruit and vegetables. In the following chapters we shall give you some delicious recipes to help you achieve this, before finally we show you how to put all of the advice together in a 28-day sample menu.

Of course it is difficult to change your eating habits – we recognize that. But with understanding and a sense of purpose you can get round any obstacle course.

5

Sauces

Considerable care must be taken about the sauces in which the fish is served. Sauces undoubtedly give colour and subtle taste to a fish meal and we are all too prone to making these very high in saturated fat by adding butter or cream. We have unfortunately lost much of that invaluable mother to daughter experience in the varied cooking of fish and fish sauces. In other countries, such as Portugal and the Basque country in Spain, where fish has remained an important part of the national diet, the traditional mouth-watering sauces are often quite different to ours. Next time you take a Portuguese or Spanish holiday, make a point of trying out different fish dishes and you will be delighted with the savoury vegetable sauces they serve. These are brightly coloured (instead of the white sauce on white fish which we favour) and have been cooked in olive or vegetable oil. Make a point of including olive oil in your meals wherever possible.

Vegetable sauces are made essentially from peeled canned tomatoes, onions, peppers, herbs, olive oil (we would recommend extra virgin olive oil), mushrooms – and, if to one's taste, garlic. It is quite easy to think up other ideas for ingredients. The key is a very juicy mix, cooked in vegetable oil. Why not experiment with the sauces yourself – try more than one with a meal at first and discover which is most to the family's tastes. When preparing a white sauce, for instance with onion or parsley, thicken with cornflour instead of using butter and plain flour. With some meals you may feel you want to add a little polyunsaturated margarine, this is fine provided you keep to your daily fat allowance. Vegetable sauces are very economical to make. The following recipes will give you some idea of what is possible. So why not try them and then invent a few of your own? Go on – make a game of experimenting and enjoy yourself.

Tomato and vegetable sauce

Serves 4

  10 ml (2 tsp) olive oil
  1 medium onion, skinned and finely chopped
  ½ green pepper, seeded and roughly chopped
  1 clove garlic, skinned and crushed (optional)
  400 g (14 oz) can chopped tomatoes
  15 ml (1 tbsp) lemon juice
  10 ml (2 tsp) dried basil
  5 ml (1 tsp) sugar
  salt and freshly ground pepper
  a little tomato purée, to thicken (optional)

Heat the oil in a saucepan and fry the onion, green pepper and garlic, if using, for a few minutes until the onion is soft and transparent. Add the tomatoes, lemon juice, basil, sugar and seasoning. Bring to the boil, reduce the heat and simmer until the sauce thickens slightly. Add a little tomato purée, if necessary.

Basque sauce with Vinho Verde

Serves 2

This sauce is usually served with sea bream but is suitable for many sea fish dishes. Allow 225 g (8 oz) fish per person.

  a little olive oil
  1 onion, skinned and finely chopped
  1 clove garlic, skinned and finely chopped
  2 large tomatoes, roughly chopped
  5 ml (1 tsp) chopped fresh parsley
  1 small red pepper, seeded and chopped
  1 glass Vinho Verde
  15 ml (1 tbsp) cornflour
  salt and freshly ground pepper

Poach the fish of your choice in a pan of water until cooked. Drain well, transfer to a serving dish and keep hot.

For the sauce, heat the oil in a saucepan and cook the onion, garlic, tomatoes, parsley and red pepper. When half cooked, add the wine and simmer until half reduced in volume. Blend the cornflour with a little water or liquid from the poached fish, then stir into the sauce. Cook over a moderate heat for about 20 minutes. Season. Strain, pour the sauce over the fish and serve.

Basque sauce cooked with fish

Serves 2

Most Basque sauces are prepared as an integral part of cooking the fish. This has many advantages, particularly in avoiding the need for adding flour to thicken. Turbot is a good choice for this recipe.

30 ml (2 tbsp) olive oil
1 small onion, skinned and finely sliced
1 clove garlic, skinned and crushed
½ green pepper, seeded and finely sliced
150 ml (¼ pint) Vinho Verde
450 g (1 lb) fish of your choice
salt and freshly ground pepper
chopped fresh parsley

To really enjoy this dish the Basque way, cook the fish in an earthenware dish.

Place the oil, onion, garlic and green pepper in a saucepan and cook slowly over a low heat for about 10 minutes, stirring occasionally. Add 30 ml (1 fl oz) wine and cook for another 3 minutes.

Place the fish in an earthenware dish, add the freshly cooked sauce and pour in the remainder of the wine. Add a little salt and pepper and sprinkle with parsley. Cook in a preheated oven at 180°C (350°F) mark 4 for 15 minutes. Remove from the oven, shake the dish gently (to bring out the gelatine), baste with sauce and cook in the oven for a further 10 minutes.

6

Soups and Starters

Children may be more reluctant than adults to make changes in their diets. Soups are a very good way of introducing them to eating fish.

Smoked fish bisque

Serves 4–6

> 225 g (8 oz) kipper fillets, skinned and chopped, or 225 g (8 oz) smoked mackerel, skinned, chopped and boned
> 400 g (14 oz) can chopped tomatoes
> 600 ml (1 pint) semi-skimmed milk
> 1 large clove garlic, skinned and crushed
> 1 medium carrot, peeled and thinly sliced
> 15 ml (1 tbsp) tomato purée
> 2.5 ml (½ tsp) anchovy essence
> 15–20 ml (1 rounded tbsp) cornflour, mixed with a little milk

Place the fish, 300–450 ml (½–¾ pint) water, tomatoes, milk, garlic and carrot in a large saucepan. Bring to the boil and simmer for 20–30 minutes. Cool slightly, then purée in a blender until smooth. Return to the pan and add the tomato purée, anchovy essence and blended cornflour. Bring back to the boil, stirring until thickened. Serve with thinly sliced, unbuttered brown bread.

Herring and vegetable soup

Serves 6

1.1 litres (2 pints) fish or chicken stock
225 g (8 oz) carrots, peeled and diced
225 g (8 oz) swede, peeled and diced
450 g (1 lb) herring fillets, diced
10 ml (2 tsp) tomato purée
salt and freshly ground pepper

Put the stock into a large saucepan. Add the carrots and swede and cook for about 20 minutes until tender. Add the fish and cook gently for 5 minutes. Allow to cool slightly. Add the tomato purée and season to taste. Purée in a blender or food processor until smooth. Return to the pan and heat until just beginning to simmer. Serve with hot crusty rolls.

Note: This soup is best made the day before and refrigerated overnight.

Smoked mackerel and fruit cocktail

Serves 4

2 smoked mackerel fillets
2 dessert apples (one red and one green), cored and diced but not peeled
15 ml (1 tbsp) lemon juice
5 cm (2 inch) piece of cucumber, diced
2 sticks of celery, sliced
125 g (4 oz) quark
225 g (8 oz) fromage frais (virtually fat-free type)
30 ml (2 tbsp) tomato ketchup
22.5 ml (1½ tbsp) Worcestershire sauce
5 ml (1 tsp) lemon juice
salt and freshly ground pepper
a few seedless grapes, to garnish

Remove the skin from the mackerel and flake the flesh. In a large bowl, toss the apples in the lemon juice. Add the mackerel pieces, cucumber and celery.

In a separate bowl, combine the quark, fromage frais, tomato ketchup, Worcestershire sauce, lemon juice and seasoning – makes 450 ml (¾ pint) sauce. Gently stir the sauce into the fish mixture. Divide between four shallow dishes and garnish with a few seedless grapes. Serve on a bed of crispy lettuce, if liked.

Note: The sauce in this recipe is very versatile. For a sweeter mixture, a little mango chutney can be added or, for a more savoury dip, add a few chopped capers.

Kipper pâté

Serves 6

4 kipper fillets
1 clove garlic, skinned and crushed
30 ml (2 tbsp) natural yogurt
5 ml (1 tsp) lemon juice
freshly ground pepper

Gently poach the kipper fillets in a saucepan of water for 4–5 minutes. Drain and remove the skin from the fillets. Chill.

Place the fish in a food processor with the garlic and process until smooth. Stir in the yogurt and lemon juice to give a smooth consistency and season with pepper. Serve with salad and wholemeal bread.

Smoked mackerel and chive pâté

Serves 4

225 g (8 oz) smoked mackerel fillet
5–10 ml (1–2 tsp) chopped fresh chives or 15 ml (1 tbsp) dried chives
5–10 ml (1–2 tsp) lemon juice
60 ml (4 tbsp) fromage frais or Greek strained yogurt
freshly ground pepper

Remove the skin and any bones from the mackerel fillets. Beat until smooth with a wooden spoon or purée in a blender. Stir in the chives, lemon juice and fromage frais or yogurt until well blended. Season with pepper. Serve with wholemeal toast and crispy raw vegetables such as celery, radishes and cucumber. This pâté is an ideal filling for sandwiches.

Smoked mackerel pâté

Serves 4

If preferred, use salmon or trout but more seasoning will be required.

175 g (6 oz) smoked mackerel fillet
juice of ½ lemon
75 g (2½ oz) low-fat cottage cheese
5 ml (1 tsp) horseradish sauce
freshly ground pepper
thin lemon slices, to garnish

Skin, bone and flake the mackerel flesh. Add the lemon juice, cheese, horseradish sauce and pepper, then mix together thoroughly. Transfer the pâté to a serving bowl and garnish with lemon slices. Chill for several hours before serving.

Kipper soup

Serves 6

450 g (1 lb) kipper fillets
2 × 400 g (14 oz) cans tomatoes
2 cloves garlic, skinned and crushed
30 ml (2 tbsp) tomato purée
150 ml (¼ pint) skimmed milk
freshly ground pepper
a little natural yogurt, to serve (optional)

Place the kippers, tails uppermost, in a tall jug, Pour on boiling water to cover and leave to stand for 5 minutes. Drain, reserving the liquid. Skin and flake the fish into a food processor. Add the tomatoes, garlic and tomato purée and blend until smooth. Pour the mixture into a large saucepan and add 450 ml (¾ pint) of the reserved liquid, together with the skimmed milk. Bring to simmering point and simmer for 5 minutes. Add pepper to taste and serve hot with a swirl of yogurt, if liked.

Salmon pâté

Serves 6

> 225 g (8 oz) cooked salmon
> 15 ml (1 tbsp) tomato purée
> 15 g (½ oz) polyunsaturated margarine
> 15 g (½ oz) plain flour
> 300 ml (½ pint) semi-skimmed milk
> 1 sachet gelatine
> salt and freshly ground pepper
> juice of ½ lemon
> 150 ml (¼ pint) natural yogurt
> thin cucumber slices, to garnish

Skin and bone the salmon, then flake the flesh. Add the tomato purée and mix thoroughly. Melt the margarine in a saucepan, add the flour and cook for 2 minutes. Remove from the heat and gradually blend in the milk. Bring to the boil and cook for 2 minutes, stirring all the time. Dissolve the gelatine in 45 ml (3 tbsp) water in a bowl over a pan of simmering water.

Add the sauce to the salmon and season well. Stir in the dissolved gelatine and allow the mixture to cool. Add the lemon juice and fold in the yogurt. Pour into a greased mould or serving dish. Chill for 3 hours before serving. Garnish with cucumber slices.

Crab and corn soup

Serves 4

600 ml (1 pint) chicken or vegetable stock
2.5 ml (½ tsp) grated fresh root ginger
15 ml (1 tbsp) cornflour
15 ml (1 tbsp) dry sherry
100 g (3½ oz) canned sweetcorn, drained
175 g (6 oz) can crabmeat
1 egg white
1 spring onion, trimmed and finely chopped, to garnish

Put the stock into a saucepan and add the ginger. Mix the cornflour with the sherry until smooth. Add the sweetcorn, then the crab with its liquid and the cornflour mixture to the stock. Bring to the boil and simmer for 2–3 minutes, stirring constantly. Turn off the heat and cover. Whisk the egg white until light and foamy, then stir into the soup. Garnish with spring onion.

Italian fish chowder

Serves 4

1 red pepper
700 g (1½ lb) tomatoes, skinned, seeded and roughly chopped
450 g (1 lb) potatoes, peeled and roughly chopped
150 ml (¼ pint) white wine
15 ml (1 tbsp) tomato purée
2 cloves garlic, skinned and crushed
5 ml (1 tsp) dried oregano
5 ml (1 tsp) dried marjoram
450 g (1 lb) firm-fleshed white fish fillet, skinned and roughly chopped
225 g (8 oz) prepared squid, cut into rings
freshly ground pepper

Cook the red pepper under the grill until the skin is charred on all sides. Allow to cool, then peel off the skin. Remove the core and seeds, then roughly chop the pepper.

Put the pepper, tomatoes, potatoes, wine, tomato purée, garlic and herbs in a large saucepan. Add 750 ml (1¼ pints) water. Cover and simmer gently for 25–30 minutes or until the potatoes are tender and the soup is thickening. Add the white fish and simmer for 10 minutes, then add the squid and cook for a further 5 minutes. Season to taste with pepper and serve immediately.

Salmon ring with cucumber and dill sauce

Serves 4

220 g (7¾ oz) can salmon, skinned and boned, liquid reserved
150 ml (¼ pint) low-fat natural yogurt
15 ml (1 tbsp) tomato purée
5 ml (1 tsp) Dijon mustard
10 ml (2 tsp) lemon juice
1 egg
60 g (2 oz) fresh wholemeal breadcrumbs
freshly ground pepper
sliced cucumber and dill leaves, to garnish

For the sauce

½ medium cucumber
2.5 ml (½ tsp) salt
150 ml (¼ pint) low-fat natural yogurt
30 ml (2 tbsp) chopped fresh dill
freshly ground pepper

Flake the salmon. Beat the yogurt, tomato purée, mustard, lemon juice, reserved salmon liquid and egg together. Stir in the flaked salmon and breadcrumbs. Season to taste. Firmly pack the mixture into a lightly greased 600 ml (1 pint) ovenproof ring mould. Cover with foil.

Place the mould in a baking tin and pour in warm water to come halfway up the mould. Bake in a preheated oven at 180°C (350°F) mark 4 for 45 minutes–1 hour or until the mixture feels firm. Leave to cool, then chill.

For the sauce, work the cucumber in a food processor until finely chopped. Put into a sieve, sprinkle with the salt and allow to drain for 30 minutes. Rinse the cucumber well under running cold water and squeeze out all the excess liquid. Transfer to a bowl and stir in the yogurt, dill and pepper to taste. Chill.

Unmould the salmon ring on to a serving plate, spoon the sauce into the centre and garnish with cucumber and dill.

Fish and prawn terrine

Serves 4

   450 g (1 lb) firm-fleshed white fish fillets, skinned
   60 ml (4 tbsp) chopped fresh dill or 30 ml (2 tbsp) dried
      dillweed
   50 ml (2 fl oz) dry white wine
   1 egg white, size 2
   freshly ground pepper
   125 g (4 oz) peeled cooked prawns, thawed if frozen, chopped
   1 small bunch watercress, finely chopped
   4 tomatoes, skinned, seeded and finely chopped
   1 clove garlic, skinned and crushed
   150 ml (¼ pint) low-fat natural yogurt
   unpeeled cooked prawns, to garnish

Purée the fish, dill, wine, egg white and seasoning in a blender or food processor until smooth. Mix the prawns and watercress together in a bowl. Spread half the fish purée in the base of a lightly oiled 450 g (1 lb) loaf tin. Sprinkle over the prawns and watercress, then spread the remaining purée over the top. Smooth with a knife, then cover with foil.

Put the loaf tin in a roasting tin with enough boiling water to come halfway up the side. Cook in a preheated oven at 200°C (400°F) mark 6 for 45 minutes or until firm. Drain off any liquid, then leave to cool for 1 hour.

Meanwhile, make the tomato sauce. Put the tomatoes and garlic in a small saucepan and simmer for 10 minutes, stirring occasionally. Mix in the yogurt and season to taste. Leave the sauce to cool.

Turn out the terrine on to a serving dish and garnish with the unpeeled cooked prawns. Cut the terrine into slices and serve with the tomato sauce.

Seafood gratin

Serves 4

    450 g (1 lb) potatoes, peeled
    300 ml (½ pint) skimmed milk, plus 45 ml (3 tbsp)
    1 slice of onion
    1 slice of carrot
    6 peppercorns
    1.25 ml (¼ tsp) ground mace
    15 g (½ oz) polyunsaturated margarine
    35 g (1¼ oz) plain flour
    salt and freshly ground pepper
    225 g (8 oz) firm fleshed white fish, skinned
    juice of ½ lemon
    90 g (3 oz) peeled prawns
    60 g (2 oz) button mushrooms, finely sliced
    30 ml (2 tbsp) grated Parmesan cheese

For the gratin, put the potatoes in a saucepan of water and cook for about 20 minutes. Drain and mash them very thoroughly with the 45 ml (3 tbsp) milk. Lightly grease four individual gratin dishes and pipe or spoon the potato around the edge. Set aside.

Put the 300 ml (½ pint) milk, onion, carrot, peppercorns and mace into a saucepan and heat until almost boiling. Allow the milk to cool, then strain into a pan. Add the margarine and flour. Heat, whisking continuously, until the sauce thickens, boils and is smooth. Simmer for 1–2 minutes. Season to taste.

Cut the fish into thin strips, divide between the dishes and pour over the lemon juice. Arrange the prawns and mushrooms over the fish. Pour over the sauce and sprinkle with Parmesan cheese. Bake in a preheated oven at 180°C (350°F) mark 4 for 20–25 minutes or until golden.

Salmon mousse

Serves 2

    15 g (½ oz) polyunsaturated margarine
    15 g (½ oz) plain flour
    150 ml (¼ pint) semi-skimmed milk
    pinch of mustard powder
    15 ml (1 tbsp) lemon juice
    pinch of cayenne pepper
    salt and freshly ground pepper
    1 egg, size 1, separated
    1 hard-boiled egg, very finely chopped
    100 g (3½ oz) can salmon, flaked, liquor reserved
    1.25 ml (¼ tsp) finely grated lemon rind
    10 ml (2 tsp) powdered gelatine
    olives and cucumber twists, to garnish

Melt the margarine in a saucepan, stir in the flour and cook for 1 minute. Remove from the heat and gradually stir in the milk. Return to the heat and bring to the boil. Add the mustard, lemon juice, cayenne and seasoning to taste. Quickly stir in the egg yolk and cook gently for 1 minute. Leave to cool.

Beat in the hard-boiled egg, salmon with its liquor and the lemon rind. Dissolve the gelatine in 30 ml (2 tbsp) water in a heatproof bowl over a pan of simmering water. Quickly stir the dissolved gelatine into the salmon mixture. Leave until on the point of setting. Beat the egg white until stiff and fold evenly into the salmon mixture. Divide between two serving dishes and chill until set. Garnish with olives and cucumber twists.

Chilled smoked trout with yogurt and orange dressing

Smoked trout is widely available at delicatessens and in most larger supermarkets. Serve as a light summer lunch with brown bread or as a starter.

Serves 4

    4 small smoked trout, skinned and filleted
    finely grated rind and juice of 1 orange
    150 ml (¼ pint) natural yogurt
    5 ml (1 tsp) creamed horseradish sauce
    salt and freshly ground pepper
    finely shredded lettuce or chicory leaves, to serve
    orange segments, to garnish

Cover the smoked trout fillets and chill for 30 minutes. Meanwhile, mix the orange rind, juice, yogurt and horse-radish together. Season to taste. Chill for at least 30 minutes with the smoked trout.

Cover four small serving plates with shredded lettuce or chicory. Carefully lay two fillets on each plate and spoon over the dressing. Garnish with orange segments and serve immediately.

Gravad lax with dill sauce

The salmon in this traditional Scandinavian dish is marinated for three days and is then ready to eat without cooking. It is usually served with dill sauce. Gravad lax can also be served in the same way as smoked salmon.

Serves 8

    15 g (½ oz) white peppercorns, coarsely crushed
    125 g (4 oz) coarse salt
    150 g (5 oz) granulated sugar
    1.8 kg (4 lb) fresh salmon, filleted
    30 g (1 oz) chopped fresh dill

For the dill sauce

    30 ml (2 tbsp) mild Swedish or German mustard
    10 ml (2 tsp) caster sugar
    1 egg yolk
    150 ml (¼ pint) olive oil
    30–45 ml (2–3 tbsp) white wine vinegar
    30 ml (2 tbsp) chopped fresh dill or 10 ml (2 tsp) dried dillweed

Mix the peppercorns with the salt and sugar. Lay one salmon fillet, skin side down, in a dish and spoon over the peppercorn mixture. Sprinkle over the dill, then place the remaining fillet on top, skin side up. Place a board on top of the fish and put weights on top to compress. Refrigerate. Turn the fish and baste with the juices daily for 3 days.

For the sauce, mix the mustard with the sugar and egg yolk. Gradually whisk in the oil, as if making mayonnaise, until the sauce is thick. Add the vinegar and dill and mix well. Keep in a cool place for at least 24 hours to allow the flavours to blend.

To serve, remove the weights, lift off the top fillet and scrape off the dill and peppercorns. Slice the salmon thinly, cutting down towards the skin across the width of the fillet. Serve with the dill sauce.

Salmon and Parma rolls

Serves 4

    50 g (2 oz) polyunsaturated margarine
    22.5 ml (1½ tbsp) chopped fresh herbs
    5 ml (1 tsp) French mustard
    freshly ground pepper
    6 slices of smoked salmon
    425 g (15 oz) can asparagus, drained and trimmed
    12 slices of Parma ham
    lemon wedges, to garnish

Blend together the margarine, herbs, mustard and pepper to taste. Cut the salmon slices in half lengthways. Spread a little of the flavoured mixture over the salmon slices. Place an asparagus spear at one end. Roll up the salmon around the asparagus to enclose it completely, letting the tip of the asparagus protrude slightly at the end of the roll. Repeat until all the salmon and half the asparagus has been used. Use the remaining asparagus to make Parma ham rolls in the same way.

Place the rolls on a serving platter, arranging them in a circle radiating out from the centre. Garnish with lemon wedges. Chill for at least 1 hour before serving.

Light Lunches and Snacks

Grilled herrings with spiced raspberry sauce

Serves 4

> 4 herrings, filleted
> a little olive oil
> 425 g (15 oz) can raspberries with juice or 250 g (8 oz) fresh or
>   frozen raspberries poached with a little water and sugar
> 10 ml (2 tsp) lemon juice
> 1.25 ml (¼ tsp) ground allspice
> cucumber twists, to garnish

Cut the fillets into diamond-shaped portions. Brush with a little olive oil and cook under a preheated medium grill for 3–4 minutes, turning once.

Purée the raspberries and push through a sieve to remove the seeds. Place in a saucepan with the lemon juice and allspice. Bring to simmering point and remove from the heat. Arrange the cooked herring pieces on a serving plate and pour a little sauce over each. Garnish with cucumber twists. Serve with a mixed salad.

Baked pickled herrings

Serves 3–4

3–4 herrings, filleted
a little plain flour
salt and freshly ground pepper
a few sliced onion rings
175 ml (6 fl oz) vinegar

Clean the insides of the fillets by rubbing with a little salt and remove the fins. Coat the fillets in the flour, seasoned with salt and pepper. Roll up and place in an ovenproof dish. Top with the onion rings. Mix the vinegar with 60 ml (2 fl oz) water and pour over the fish. Cover and bake in a preheated oven at 180°C (350°F) mark 4 for about 35 minutes, removing the lid about 10 minutes before the end of the cooking time to brown slightly. Allow to cool, then serve with salad and wholemeal bread.

Stir-fried herrings and vegetables

Serves 4

4 × 175 g (6 oz) herring fillets
30 ml (2 tbsp) dry sherry
15 ml (1 tbsp) soy sauce
10 ml (2 tsp) olive oil
60 g (2 oz) fennel, sliced
1 small red pepper, seeded and sliced
1 small bunch spring onions, trimmed and sliced

Slice the herrings into 2.5 cm (1 inch) pieces. Marinate in the sherry and soy sauce for 1 hour. Heat the oil in a large frying pan or wok until quite hot. Quickly stir-fry the fennel and pepper for 1–2 minutes. Add the spring onions and herrings with the marinade and cook over a high heat, stirring continuously. Serve with brown rice.

Note: A few sliced water chestnuts or bamboo shoots can also be added at the same time as the herrings.

Tomato herrings

Serves 4

> 5 ml (1 tsp) olive oil
> ½ small onion, skinned and chopped
> 4 herrings, filleted
> 200 g (7 oz) can chopped tomatoes
> 15 ml (1 tbsp) lemon juice
> 5 ml (1 tsp) dried basil
> 2.5 ml (½ tsp) sugar
> salt and freshly ground pepper

Heat the oil in a large shallow pan and cook the onion until soft and transparent. Add the herring fillets and cook for 2 minutes over a gentle heat. Turn the fillets over, add the tomatoes, lemon juice, basil, sugar and seasoning, cover and simmer for 4–5 minutes. Serve with warm wholemeal pitta bread or crusty granary rolls.

Kipper stir-fry

If using frozen boil-in-the-bag kippers for this recipe, defrost and remove the butter first.

Serves 4

> 15 ml (1 tbsp) olive oil
> 1 clove garlic, skinned and finely chopped
> 1 medium onion, skinned and thinly sliced
> 1 red pepper, seeded and thinly sliced
> 1 green pepper, seeded and thinly sliced
> 175 g (6 oz) Chinese leaves or white cabbage, shredded
> 225 g (8 oz) skinned kipper fillets
> 200 g (7 oz) can sweetcorn, drained
> freshly ground pepper
> 60 ml (4 tbsp) whisky

Heat the oil in a large frying pan or wok and cook the garlic and onion until soft and transparent. Stir in the peppers and Chinese leaves and cook for a further 2 minutes. Stir in the kippers and cook for 4 minutes, stirring carefully. Add the sweetcorn, pepper and whisky. Cook for a further 2 minutes, then flambé. Serve immediately with brown rice or Chinese noodles.

Moules à la bordelaise

Mussels should have a fresh, salty smell. When buying, check that each shell is tightly closed, or closes when tapped – indicating that the mussels are still alive. During cooking, all the shells should open up – any that remain closed must be discarded. This dish makes an excellent lunch or starter.

Serves 4

> 2.5 litres (4 pints) mussels
> 120 ml (4 fl oz) dry white wine
> 30 ml (1 fl oz) olive oil
> 1 medium onion, skinned and finely chopped
> 1 clove garlic, skinned and chopped
> 450 g (1 lb) tomatoes, skinned, seeded and chopped
> 45 ml (3 tbsp) chopped fresh parsley
> grated rind of ½ lemon
> salt and freshly ground pepper
> 90 g (3 oz) fresh wholemeal breadcrumbs

To prepare the mussels, scrub them under cold running water. Scrape off any barnacles and pull away the wiry beard which sprouts between each shell.

Place the mussels and wine in a large pan, cover and leave over a high heat until they have opened. Discard any that remain closed. Strain the mussels, remove the empty shells and reserve the cooking liquid.

Heat the olive oil in a pan and fry the onion and garlic for 2 minutes. Add the tomatoes, parsley, lemon rind and seasoning and stir in the reserved liquid to enable the tomatoes to simmer until cooked. The finished sauce will be quite thin. Arrange the mussels in a large flameproof dish. Pour over the sauce and sprinkle with breadcrumbs. Cook under a preheated moderate grill until golden.

Mackerel and potato salad

Serves 4

> 225 g (8 oz) smoked mackerel fillets, boned and cubed
> 300 g (10 oz) can broad beans, drained
> 350 g (12 oz) new potatoes, scrubbed and cooked in their skins
>   or 300 g (10 oz) can potatoes, drained
> 150 ml (¼ pint) natural yogurt
> 5 ml (1 tsp) creamed horseradish
> freshly ground pepper
> chopped fresh parsley, to garnish

Mix the mackerel and broad beans together. Slice the cold
potatoes and arrange in an overlapping circle on each plate.
Put a quarter of the mackerel and bean mixture in the centre
of the potatoes. Blend the yogurt, horseradish and pepper
together and pour over the salad. Garnish with parsley.

Moules à la marinière

This mouthwatering seafood dish makes an excellent lunch
or starter.

Serves 6

> 3.5 litres (6 pints) mussels
> 300 ml (½ pint) dry white wine
> 15 ml (1 tbsp) olive oil
> 1 onion, skinned and finely chopped
> 1 bay leaf
> 2 thyme sprigs
> 45 ml (3 tbsp) chopped fresh parsley
> freshly ground pepper

Prepare the mussels as for Moules à la bordelaise (p. 79).
Put all the ingredients, except the mussels, parsley and
pepper into a large pan with a close-fitting lid. Bring them
to a fierce boil and drop all the mussels in together. Cover
the pan tightly so that a good head of steam builds up
inside. Keep the heat high for 5 minutes, periodically giving

the pan a good shake. Remove the lid and, if the mussels have opened, they are ready. If not, give them a minute or so longer. Discard any that remain closed.

Strain the cooking liquid into a warmed jug. Spoon the mussels into serving bowls and pour the liquid over them. Sprinkle with parsley and pepper.

Mackerel baked potatoes

Serves 2

225 g (8 oz) smoked mackerel fillets, skinned
15 ml (1 tbsp) horseradish sauce (optional)
salt and freshly ground pepper
a little skimmed milk
2 x 225 g (8 oz) potatoes, baked in the oven
30 g (1 oz) low- to medium-fat cheese, grated

Flake the mackerel into a bowl and mix in the horseradish sauce, if using, seasoning and a little milk. Cut open the potatoes and fill with the fish mixture. Cook under a preheated medium grill until the mackerel is hot. Sprinkle over the cheese and return to the grill until the cheese has melted. Serve hot with a mixed salad.

Crab and rice salad

Serves 2

175 g (6 oz) long grain rice
salt and freshly ground pepper
150 g (5 oz) canned crabmeat
½ green pepper, seeded and chopped
½ red pepper, seeded and chopped
90 g (3 oz) stoned black olives
1 stick of celery, thinly sliced
60 g (2 oz) button mushrooms, sliced
30 g (1 oz) walnuts, chopped (optional)

For the dressing

    45–60 ml (3–4 tbsp) olive oil
    juice of 1 lemon
    salt and freshly ground pepper

Cook the rice in a saucepan of boiling salted water for about 15 minutes or until tender, then drain and rinse with boiling water. Leave to drain and dry a little. Mix the dressing ingredients together, then stir well into the rice while the rice is still warm. Leave to cool.

Meanwhile, flake the crabmeat and mix with the peppers, olives, celery, mushrooms, seasoning and walnuts, if using. When the rice is cold, combine with the crab and vegetable mixture.

Sardine and tomato pizza

Serves 2

For the base

    125 g (4 oz) self raising flour
    salt and freshly ground pepper
    30 g (1 oz) polyunsaturated margarine
    10 ml (2 tsp) dried mixed herbs
    1 egg, beaten
    a little semi-skimmed milk

For the topping

    15 ml (1 tbsp) olive oil
    1 small onion, skinned and sliced
    2 tomatoes, skinned and sliced
    125 g (4 oz) can sardines in tomato sauce
    60 g (2 oz) Mozzarella cheese, grated
    salt and freshly ground pepper
    chopped fresh parsley, to garnish

For the base, sift the flour into a bowl with a little seasoning. Rub in the margarine until the mixture resembles fine breadcrumbs. Add the herbs, egg and enough milk to make fairly soft dough. Shape into a round, about 15 cm (6 inches), and place on a lightly oiled baking sheet.

Heat the olive oil in a frying pan and fry the onion until soft. Spread over the dough. Cover with the tomato slices, then the sardines with tomato sauce, finishing with the cheese. Bake in a preheated oven at 230°C (450°F) mark 8 for 15–20 minutes until the pizza is well risen and the cheese slightly brown. Serve hot, garnished with parsley.

Golden fish quiche

Serves 4–6

For the pastry

90 g (3 oz) plain flour
90 g (3 oz) wholemeal flour
90 g (3 oz) polyunsaturated margarine

For the filling

225 g (8 oz) whiting or coley fillet, skinned and cubed
225 g (8 oz) smoked haddock fillet, skinned and cubed
60 g (2 oz) peas
2 eggs
300 ml (½ pint) semi-skimmed milk
salt and freshly ground pepper

For the pastry, mix the flours together in a bowl. Rub in the margarine until the mixture resembles fine breadcrumbs. Stir in enough water to make a dough. Roll out and use to line a 20 cm (8 inch) flan ring or dish.

For the filling, mix the fish and peas together and spoon into the pastry case. Beat the eggs, milk and seasoning together and pour over the fish. Bake in a preheated oven at 200°C (400°F) mark 6 for 35–40 minutes until golden. Serve with plenty of mixed salad.

Herring with red peppers

Serves 2–4

4 herrings, cleaned and boned
1 large red pepper, seeded and cut into squares

For the marinade

45 ml (3 tbsp) olive oil
grated rind and juice of 1 orange
grated rind and juice of 1 lemon
chopped fresh thyme or parsley
salt and freshly ground pepper

Cut each herring into four crosswise. Thread the herring and red pepper alternately on to four short skewers. Combine all the marinade ingredients and brush over the fish. Cook under a preheated grill for about 10 minutes, basting with the marinade and turning the skewers frequently. Serve with sweetcorn and mixed peppers or rice.

Prawn stir-fry

Serves 4–6

15 ml (1 tbsp) olive oil
1 onion, skinned and thinly sliced
1 clove garlic, skinned and crushed
1 cm (½ inch) piece of fresh root ginger, peeled and thinly sliced
2 carrots, peeled and thinly sliced
1 small green pepper, seeded and thinly sliced
60 g (2 oz) Chinese leaves, shredded
60 g (2 oz) beanshoots
375 g (13 oz) peeled prawns
15 ml (1 tbsp) soy sauce
freshly ground pepper

Heat the oil in a wok or large frying pan and stir-fry the onion, garlic and ginger, stirring constantly. Add the carrots and green pepper. After a few minutes, stir in the Chinese leaves and beanshoots. Stirring continuously, add the prawns, soy sauce and black pepper. Continue cooking and stirring for 2–3 minutes until the prawns are hot. Serve immediately with brown rice or wholewheat noodles.

Pasta with hot tuna sauce

Serves 4

300 ml (½ pint) chopped tomatoes
1 large red pepper, seeded and sliced
1 onion, skinned and chopped
1 clove garlic, skinned and finely chopped
5 ml (1 tsp) dried oregano
pinch of chilli powder
150 ml (¼ pint) vegetable stock or water
350 g (12 oz) pasta shapes or macaroni, preferably wholewheat
200 g (7 oz) can tuna, drained and flaked
30 g (1 oz) stoned black olives
salt and freshly ground pepper
a little Parmesan cheese, to serve

Place the tomatoes, pepper, onion, garlic, oregano and chilli powder in a saucepan. Bring to the boil, cover and simmer until the vegetables are tender. Allow to cool a little, then purée in a blender or food processor.

Meanwhile, cook the pasta according to the instructions on the packet. Return the puréed mixture to the saucepan, add the tuna and olives and heat through. Season. Serve with the hot pasta and a little grated Parmesan cheese.

Crisp and crunchy plaice salad

Serves 4

450 g (1 lb) plaice fillets, skinned and cut into strips
15 ml (1 tbsp) lemon juice
salt and freshly ground pepper
½ melon, peeled, seeded and cubed
6 small radishes
2 sticks of celery, sliced
½ iceberg lettuce, shredded

For the dressing

> 15 ml (1 tbsp) white wine vinegar
> 45 ml (3 tbsp) olive oil
> 15 ml (1 tbsp) chopped fresh dill

Poach the plaice in 150 ml (¼ pint) water with the lemon juice and seasoning added. Drain and chill. Carefully mix chilled fish with the remaining ingredients.

For the dressing, put all the ingredients in a screwtop jar and shake well. Pour over the salad and toss lightly.

Caerphilly and crabmeat flan

Serves 4–6

For the pastry

> 90 g (3 oz) plain flour
> 90 g (3 oz) wholemeal flour
> 45 g (1½ oz) polyunsaturated margarine

For the filling

> 225 g (8 oz) brown and white crabmeat, fresh or defrosted
> 5 ml (1 tsp) Dijon mustard
> 2 eggs, beaten
> 150 ml (¼ pint) semi-skimmed milk
> salt and freshly ground pepper
> 30 g (1 oz) Caerphilly cheese
> 2.5 ml (½ tsp) paprika

For the pastry, combine the flours in a bowl. Rub in the margarine until the mixture resembles fine breadcrumbs. Stir in enough water to make a dough. Roll out and use to line a 20 cm (8 inch) flan tin.

For the filling, mix brown and white crab meat together and beat in mustard, eggs, milk and seasoning. Pour into the pastry case and crumble over the cheese. Sprinkle with paprika and place on a baking sheet. Bake in a preheated oven at 200°C (400°F) mark 6 for 35–40 minutes until golden brown. Serve hot or cold with a crisp green salad.

Dill-marinated herrings

Serves 4–6

150 ml (¼ pint) sherry
150 ml (¼ pint) white wine vinegar
30 ml (2 tbsp) Worcestershire sauce
15 ml (1 tbsp) light brown sugar
2 dill sprigs, chopped or 15 ml (1 tbsp) dried dillweed
30 ml (2 tbsp) soured cream
4 × 175–225 g (6–8 oz) herring fillets, skinned if preferred
150 ml (¼ pint) low-fat natural yogurt
5 cm (2 inch) piece of cucumber

Mix the sherry, vinegar, Worcestershire sauce and sugar together in a pan. Bring to the boil, then allow to cool. Add the dill and, when the liquid has completely cooled, add the soured cream. Mix well.

Cut the herring fillets into 5 cm (2 inch) strips and place in a glass dish. Cover with the dill marinade and refrigerate for at least 48 hours.

Mix the yogurt and cucumber together. Drain the marinade from the fish and serve the marinated fish with yogurt and cucumber sauce. Serve with a mixed salad and warm wholemeal rolls.

Oily Fish Main Meals

Cucumber cream (for salmon steaks)

½ cucumber, grated
125 g (4 oz) curd cheese, softened
30 ml (2 tbsp) lemon juice
30 ml (2 tbsp) semi-skimmed milk
15 ml (1 tbsp) chopped fresh parsley
salt and freshly ground pepper
lemon slices and parsley, to garnish

Blend all ingredients together, then spoon over salmon steaks.

Roast Scottish salmon with paprika sauce

This makes a wonderful alternative Sunday lunch.

Serves 4

4 x 150 g (5 oz) tail piece fillets of salmon
120 ml (4 fl oz) dry white wine

For the topping

30 g (1 oz) fresh breadcrumbs
5 ml (1 tsp) paprika
5 ml (1 tsp) chopped fresh dill
salt and freshly ground pepper
30 g (1 oz) polyunsaturated margarine

For the sauce

2.5 ml (½ tsp) paprika
150 ml (¼ pint) fish stock
2.5 ml (½ tsp) cornflour

Place the salmon fillets in a roasting dish and pour the wine over. For the topping, mix the breadcrumbs, paprika and dill with a little seasoning. Scatter over the fish, then dot with the margarine. Bake in a preheated oven at 200°C (400°F) mark 6 for 15 minutes. Lift the fish on to warmed serving plates and keep warm.

For the sauce, pour the fish cooking juices into a pan and add the paprika and stock. Simmer for 2–3 minutes to reduce a little. Blend the cornflour with 15 ml (1 tbsp) water, whisk into the sauce and heat until thickened. Pour around the salmon and serve.

Scottish salmon en papillote

Serves 4

2 medium carrots, peeled and cut into julienne strips
1 yellow pepper, seeded and cut into thin slices
1 medium leek, trimmed, washed and finely shredded
4 × 175 g (6 oz) salmon steaks or cutlets
juice of 2 medium oranges
45 ml (3 tbsp) soy sauce
4 spring onions, trimmed and chopped
orange twists, to garnish

Mix the carrots, yellow pepper and leek together. Divide between 4 × 45 cm (18 inch) squares of greaseproof paper or baking parchment. Place a salmon steak on each pile of vegetables. Mix the orange juice and soy sauce together. Spoon over the salmon and sprinkle over the spring onions. Bring the sides of the paper to the centre and fold together. Taper the ends and fold under the salmon to make a neat parcel. Either microwave on HIGH for 4½–5 minutes or place in a steamer and cook for 8–10 minutes or until the salmon is cooked. Garnish with orange twists and serve with rice or baked potatoes and vegetables.

Scottish salmon with cucumber and tomato sauces

Serves 4

4 x 150 g (5 oz) salmon steaks

For the cucumber sauce

½ cucumber, roughly chopped
salt and freshly ground pepper
90 g (3 oz) fromage frais or quark
5 ml (1 tsp) white wine vinegar

For the tomato sauce

4 ripe tomatoes, skinned and seeded
10 ml (2 tsp) olive oil
5 ml (1 tsp) white wine vinegar
salt and freshly ground pepper
chopped fresh chives
2.5 ml (½ tsp) ready-made mustard

For the cucumber sauce, place the cucumber in a colander, sprinkle with salt and leave for 30 minutes. Rinse and dry on absorbent kitchen paper. Put into a blender with the rest of the ingredients and blend until finely chopped.

For the tomato sauce, purée the tomatoes in a blender. In a clean screwtop jar, combine the oil, vinegar, seasoning, chives and mustard. Add to the tomatoes and mix well.

Place the salmon steaks on a foil-lined grill pan or baking sheet and cook under a preheated hot grill for 3 minutes each side.

Serve the salmon steaks with a little of each sauce and accompany with boiled new potatoes and seasonal vegetables and/or mixed salad.

Salmon and prawn tagliatelle

Serves 4

45 g (1½ oz) polyunsaturated margarine
1 small onion, skinned and thinly sliced
45 g (1½ oz) plain flour
300 ml (½ pint) semi-skimmed milk
150 ml (¼ pint) fish stock
salt and freshly ground pepper
175 g (6 oz) button mushrooms, sliced
125 g (4 oz) peeled prawns
350 g (12 oz) cold cooked salmon, skinned and flaked
225 g (8 oz) green tagliatelle

Melt the margarine in a large pan and cook the onion until soft and transparent. Stir in the flour and cook for 1–2 minutes. Remove from the heat and gradually stir in the milk. Return to the heat and cook, stirring constantly, until the sauce is thickened and smooth. Reduce the heat and gradually stir in the fish stock. Season and stir in the mushrooms. Simmer gently, stirring occasionally, for about 2 minutes. Stir in the prawns and salmon and continue cooking for 1–2 minutes or until the prawns and salmon are hot.

Meanwhile, cook the tagliatelle according to the packet instructions. Drain and serve with the fish sauce.

Grilled mackerel with sage sauce

A delicious, quick and easy way to serve mackerel.

Serves 4

4 mackerel, cleaned
salt and freshly ground pepper
150 ml (¼ pint) olive oil
30 ml (2 tbsp) lemon juice
75 ml (3 fl oz) dry white wine
75 ml (3 fl oz) dry vermouth
5 ml (1 tsp) very finely chopped fresh sage

Cut the fins from the mackerel, then cut three diagonal slits in the skin across both sides of the fish. Season the fish inside and out, then place in a dish large enough to hold them in a single layer. Mix the oil, lemon juice and wine together and pour over the fish. Cover and leave to marinate in a cool place for 1½ hours, turning the fish occasionally.

Remove the mackerel from the marinade. Cook under a preheated hot grill for 5–8 minutes on each side, depending on the thickness of the fish, until the flesh flakes easily. Transfer to a warmed serving dish, cover and keep hot. Carefully remove the oil from the top of the marinade. Pour the marinade and any cooking juices into a saucepan, add the vermouth and sage and simmer for 2–3 minutes. Season to taste and pour over the mackerel.

Baked trout with dill

Serves 4

> 4 x 300 g (10 oz) trout, cleaned
> 40 ml (8 tsp) lemon juice
> salt and freshly ground pepper
> 4 dill sprigs
> 120 ml (4 fl oz) dry white wine
> 1 shallot, skinned and finely chopped
> lemon slices and dill sprigs, to garnish

Cut the fins from the fish, then sprinkle 30 ml (6 tsp) of the lemon juice over the skin and the cavities. Season inside and out and put a sprig of dill in each cavity. Place the trout in a baking dish large enough to hold them tightly in one layer. Pour over the wine and add the shallot. Cover the dish with greased greaseproof paper. Bake in a preheated oven at 180°C (350°F) mark 4 for 20–25 minutes or until the flesh flakes easily.

Carefully transfer the trout to four warmed serving plates and keep warm. Pour the juices into a saucepan with the remaining lemon juice and boil rapidly until reduced to about 60 ml (4 tbsp). Spoon over the fish and serve immediately garnished with lemon slices and dill sprigs.

Salmon kedgeree

Serves 6

350 g (12 oz) salmon
150 ml (¼ pint) dry white wine
2 small onions, skinned and chopped
1 carrot, peeled and sliced
1 stick celery, chopped
15 ml (1 tbsp) lemon juice
6 peppercorns
1 bouquet garni
salt and freshly ground pepper
350 g (12 oz) long grain rice
60 g (2 oz) polyunsaturated margarine
7.5 ml (1½ tsp) English mustard powder
3 hard-boiled eggs, quartered
cayenne
parsley sprigs, to garnish

Put the salmon in a saucepan, pour in the wine and enough water to cover the fish. Add half of the chopped onion, the carrot, celery, lemon juice, peppercorns, bouquet garni and 5 ml (1 tsp) salt. Bring slowly to the boil, then remove from the heat. Cover tightly and cool.

Cook the rice in a saucepan of boiling salted water for 15–20 minutes until tender.

Meanwhile, remove the salmon from the liquid and flake the flesh, discarding skin and any bones. Strain the cooking liquid and reserve. Melt 30 g (1 oz) of the margarine in a large frying pan and gently fry the remaining onion until soft. Drain the rice thoroughly, then add to the onion with the remaining margarine. Toss gently to coat in the margarine, then stir in the mustard powder. Add the flaked salmon, hard-boiled eggs and a few spoonfuls of the strained cooking liquid to moisten. Heat through. Shake the pan and toss the ingredients gently so that the salmon and eggs do not break up.

Transfer to a warmed serving dish and sprinkle with cayenne to taste. Serve immediately, garnished with parsley.

Mackerel fillets in oatmeal and almonds

Serves 4

> 2 whole mackerel, each weighing about 550 g (1¼ lb), cleaned
> 30 ml (2 tbsp) plain flour, seasoned with salt and pepper
> 90 g (3 oz) whole almonds
> 125 g (4 oz) coarse oatmeal
> 1 egg, lightly beaten
> juice of 1 orange

Cut the heads off the mackerel. Using a sharp knife, split the fish open all the way along the underside. Place the fish flesh-side down on a board and press firmly all along the backbone to loosen the bone and flatten the fish. Turn the fish flesh side up and ease out the backbone. Cut each fish in half to give two fillets then, if wished, carefully skin each one. (A good fishmonger will do this for you.)

Coat each fillet lightly in the seasoned flour. Blanch the almonds in boiling water for about 1 minute. Pop them out of their skins and finely chop. Place in a shallow dish with the oatmeal. Dip each fillet of mackerel into the egg, then coat in the nuts and oatmeal. Place on a baking sheet. Squeeze a little orange juice over each fillet. Cook under a preheated grill for about 5 minutes each side. Serve immediately, accompanied by a watercress and orange salad and boiled new potatoes.

Mackerel fillets with mushrooms

Serves 4

> 4 mackerel fillets
> 175 g (6 oz) mushrooms, quartered
> 30 ml (2 tbsp) lemon juice
> salt and freshly ground pepper

Place the mackerel fillets, skin side down, in an ovenproof dish. Sprinkle over the mushrooms, lemon juice and seasoning. Cover and bake in a preheated oven at 190°C (375°F) mark 5 for 25–30 minutes. Serve with mashed potatoes, grilled tomatoes and peas.

Salade Niçoise

Serves 4

    175 g (6 oz) small new potatoes, scrubbed and halved
    salt and freshly ground pepper
    198 g (7 oz) can tuna in brine, drained
    225 g (8 oz) tomatoes, quartered
    60 g (2 oz) black olives, stoned
    ½ small cucumber, thinly sliced
    225 g (8 oz) cooked French beans
    3 hard-boiled eggs, quartered
    ½ iceberg lettuce, cut into chunks
    8 anchovy fillets, drained and halved
    30 ml (2 tbsp) chopped fresh parsley

For the dressing

    90 ml (6 tbsp) olive oil
    30 ml (2 tbsp) white wine vinegar
    15 ml (1 tbsp) lemon juice
    15 ml (1 tbsp) mild wholegrain mustard
    large pinch of sugar
    salt and freshly ground pepper

Cook the potatoes in a saucepan of boiling salted water until tender. Meanwhile, for the dressing, whisk together the oil, vinegar, lemon juice, mustard and sugar. Season. Drain the potatoes and toss in the dressing. Leave to cool, stirring occasionally.

Flake the tuna into large chunks. Arrange in a bowl with the tomatoes, olives, cucumber, beans, eggs, lettuce and cold dressed potatoes. Sprinkle with anchovies and parsley.

Trout poached in wine

Serves 4

    4 trout, cleaned
    salt and freshly ground pepper
    60 g (2 oz) polyunsaturated margarine
    1 large onion, skinned and sliced
    2 sticks celery, sliced
    2 carrots, peeled and very thinly sliced
    300 ml (½ pint) dry white wine
    1 bouquet garni
    15 ml (1 tbsp) plain flour
    lemon wedges and chopped fresh parsley, to garnish

Season the insides of the trout. Melt 45 g (1½ oz) of the margarine in a small saucepan and add the onion, celery and carrots. Stir well to coat with the margarine. Cover and sweat for 5 minutes over a very low heat. Lay the vegetables in an oiled casserole and arrange the fish on top. Pour over the wine and add the bouquet garni.

Cover tightly and cook in a preheated oven at 180°C (350°F) mark 4 for about 25 minutes or until the trout are cooked. Transfer to a warmed serving dish and keep hot. Pour the cooking juices into a small pan, discarding the bouquet garni. Blend together the remaining margarine and the flour. Whisk into the sauce and simmer gently, stirring, until thickened. Pour into a jug. Garnish the fish with lemon and parsley and serve with the sauce.

Spiced halibut steaks

Serves 4

    60 ml (4 tbsp) olive oil
    1 small onion, skinned and finely chopped
    15 g (½ oz) fresh green and red chillies, seeded and sliced
    10 ml (2 tsp) curry powder
    2.5 ml (½ tsp) ground cumin
    30 ml (2 tbsp) lemon juice
    4 x 225 g (8 oz) halibut steaks
    salt and freshly ground pepper

Heat the oil in a frying pan and fry the onion and chillies with the spices for 2–3 minutes. Add the lemon juice. Place the halibut steaks in shallow ovenproof dish and brush the spice mixture over the fish. Cover and leave to marinate in the refrigerator for 1–2 hours.

Place the steaks on a grill pan, season and cook under a preheated moderate to hot grill for 10–12 minutes, brushing with the remaining marinade. Serve hot with vegetables.

Mackerel with orange sauce

Serves 4

1 very large or 2 medium mackerel, about 1 kg (2 lb), cleaned
2 small leeks, trimmed, washed and cut into matchstick strips
2 sticks celery, cut into matchstick strips
juice of 2 oranges
thinly pared rind of 1 orange
2 red or yellow peppers
5 ml (1 tsp) green peppercorns, crushed
salt and freshly ground pepper

Leave the head and tail on the mackerel. Scatter the leeks and celery over the base of a roasting tin and place the fish on top. Pour the orange juice over the fish. Cover the tin with foil and bake in a preheated oven at 190°C (375°F) mark 5 for 25–40 minutes or until the fish flakes easily when tested with a fork.

Meanwhile, cut the pared orange rind into very thin strips. Blanch in a saucepan of boiling water for 4–5 minutes, then drain and set aside.

Put the peppers under a preheated hot grill and char the skins quickly all over. Cool slightly, then peel. Discard the core and seeds, then finely chop the pepper. Put the pepper and 200 ml (⅓ pint) water in a saucepan and cook until very tender and almost all the water has evaporated.

When the fish is cooked, strain the juices into the pan with the peppers, reserving the vegetables. Purée the sauce in a blender or food processor and return to the pan. Add the peppercorns and seasoning, then cook for a further minute. Serve the mackerel garnished with the vegetables and orange rind. Serve the sauce separately.

Trout with almond topping

Serves 4

15 g (½ oz) polyunsaturated margarine
30 ml (2 tbsp) chopped fresh parsley
50 ml (2 fl oz) dry white vermouth
4 trout, each weighing about 350 g (12 oz), cleaned and boned
salt and freshly ground pepper
60 g (2 oz) fresh wholemeal breadcrumbs
60 g (2 oz) blanched almonds, chopped
parsley sprigs, to garnish

Grease a large ovenproof dish with a little of the margarine.
Scatter over the parsley and pour in the vermouth. Open
out the trout and place, skin side down, in a single layer in
the dish. Season to taste. Combine the breadcrumbs and
almonds. Spread evenly over the fish. Dot with the remaining margarine.

Cook in a preheated oven at 190°C (375°F) mark 5 for 20
minutes or until the topping is crisp and the fish flakes
easily when tested with a fork. Garnish with parsley.

Parchment-baked salmon

For maximum flavour, soak the parchment in wine. This
very convenient way of baking salmon produces excellent
moist results.

Serves 4

30 ml (2 fl oz) dry white wine
125 g (4 oz) cucumber, thinly sliced
4 salmon steaks, about 150 g (5 oz) each
15 ml (1 tbsp) fennel seeds or 2.5 ml (½ tsp) dried dill seeds
30 g (1 oz) polyunsaturated margarine
salt and freshly ground pepper
fresh dill, to garnish

Cut four pieces of non-stick parchment or greaseproof
paper about 27.5 cm (11 inches) square. Crush the pieces of
parchment together into a flattish round. Place in a small

bowl and pour over the wine. Leave to soak for 1 hour. Push down into the wine occasionally.

Separate and open out the parchment sheets. Arrange a circle of cucumber slices in the centre of each sheet. Place a salmon steak on top. Sprinkle with fennel or dill seeds and top with a small piece of margarine. Season to taste. Drizzle any remaining white wine over the salmon.

Lift up the opposite sides of the parchment and fold together. Twist and tuck under the two shorter ends. Place the parcels on a baking sheet. Bake in a preheated oven at 200°C (400°F) mark 6 for about 15 minutes. Garnish with fresh dill and serve immediately straight from the parchment. Serve with boiled new potatoes and a green salad.

Lentil tuna savoury

Serves 4

175 g (6 oz) red lentils, rinsed
15 g (½ oz) polyunsaturated margarine
1 small onion, skinned and finely chopped
175 g (6 oz) tuna steak, cooked, or 198 g (7 oz) can tuna, drained
1 egg, size 1
150 ml (¼ pint) semi-skimmed milk
salt and freshly ground pepper
30 g (1 oz) salted peanuts, finely chopped

Place the lentils in a saucepan with 600 ml (1 pint) water. Bring to the boil, then simmer for 20–25 minutes until the lentils are just tender and most of the liquid has evaporated, stirring occasionally.

Melt the margarine in a saucepan and gently fry the onion without colouring until softened. Meanwhile, roughly flake the tuna. Remove the pan of onion from the heat and stir in the tuna. Beat the lentils, egg and milk into the tuna mixture. Season to taste. Spoon into a shallow 1 litre (2 pint) ovenproof dish. Sprinkle the peanuts over the dish. Bake in a preheated oven at 180°C (350°F) mark 4 for 20–30 minutes.

Italian marinated trout

Serves 4

> 4 whole trout, about 225 g (8 oz) each, cleaned with heads on
> 30 ml (2 tbsp) plain flour
> 30 ml (2 tbsp) olive oil
> 1 small bulb Florence fennel, trimmed and finely sliced
> 1 medium onion, skinned and finely sliced
> 300 ml (½ pint) Italian dry white wine
> finely grated rind and juice of 1 orange
> salt and freshly ground pepper
> chopped fennel tops
> orange slices, to garnish

Dip the trout in the flour. Heat the oil in a frying pan and fry the fish gently for 4 minutes on each side. Using a fish slice, transfer the fish to a shallow dish. With a sharp knife, score the skin diagonally, being careful not to cut into the flesh.

Add the fennel and onion to the frying pan and fry for 5 minutes. Add the wine, orange rind and juice and seasoning to taste. Bring to the boil and boil rapidly for 1 minute. Add the chopped fennel tops and pour immediately over the fish. Leave the trout to cool completely in the marinade.

Marinate in the refrigerator for at least 8 hours, but no more than three days. Serve at room temperature, garnished with orange slices.

Tarragon stuffed trout

Serves 6

> 6 rainbow trout, about 225 g (8 oz) each, cleaned with heads on

For the stuffing

> 125 g (4 oz) peeled prawns
> 30 ml (2 tbsp) olive oil
> 1 medium onion, skinned and finely chopped
> 225 g (8 oz) button mushrooms, roughly chopped
> 5 ml (1 tsp) chopped fresh tarragon or 1.25 ml (¼ tsp)
>   dried tarragon

salt and freshly ground pepper
30 g (1 oz) long grain rice, cooked
30 ml (2 tbsp) lemon juice
tarragon sprigs, to garnish

For the stuffing, cut each prawn into two or three pieces. Melt the oil in a large frying pan and fry the onion for 5 minutes until golden brown. Add the mushrooms with the tarragon and seasoning to taste. Cook over a high heat for 5–10 minutes until all excess moisture has evaporated. Leave to cool for about 30 minutes. Carefully mix the prawns, rice, lemon juice and mushroom mixture together and adjust the seasoning.

Place the fish side by side in a lightly oiled ovenproof dish and stuff each with the mixture. Cover and cook in a preheated oven at 180°C (350°F) mark 4 for about 30 minutes or until cooked. Serve garnished with tarragon. Accompany with boiled new potatoes and mange tout or petits pois.

Argyll salmon with oranges and pasta

Serves 4

450 g (1 lb) Scottish salmon fillets, skinned
225 g (8 oz) tagliatelle or fettuccine
4 large onions
15 ml (1 tbsp) cornflour
4 spring onions, trimmed and sliced
freshly ground pepper
parsley sprigs, to garnish

Cut the salmon into strips about 1 cm (½ inch) wide. Cook the pasta in a saucepan of boiling salted water until just tender.

Meanwhile, using a sharp knife, cut all the peel and white pith away from two of the oranges and carefully remove the segments, catching the juice in a bowl. Squeeze the juice from two oranges and, if necessary, make up to 225 ml (8 fl oz) with cold water. Blend the cornflour with

45 ml (3 tbsp) juice and leave to one side. Place the remaining juice in a wide saucepan. Bring almost to the boil, add the salmon strips and poach gently for 2–3 minutes. Lift out carefully with a draining spoon and keep hot.

Stir the spring onions and blended cornflour into the pan and heat until boiling. Cook, stirring, for 1 minute, then season with pepper. Add the salmon and orange segments. Drain the pasta, spoon the salmon mixture over and serve garnished with parsley sprigs.

Highland ginger steaks with herb rice

Serves 4

>   4 Scottish salmon steaks, about 175 g (6 oz) each
>   5 ml (1 tsp) ground ginger
>   15 ml (1 tbsp) olive or vegetable oil
>   30 ml (2 tbsp) dry sherry
>   15 ml (1 tbsp) clear honey

For the herb rice

>   225 g (8 oz) long grain rice
>   salt and freshly ground pepper
>   finely grated rind of 1 lemon
>   45 ml (3 tbsp) chopped fresh chervil or parsley
>   lemon slices and fresh herbs, to garnish

Place the salmon in a shallow dish. Mix together the ginger, oil, sherry and honey. Pour evenly over the salmon, cover and chill for about 1 hour.

Cook the rice in a large saucepan of boiling lightly salted water for 12–15 minutes or until tender.

Meanwhile, cook the salmon under a preheated moderate grill for 7–8 minutes, turning once, brushing with the marinade to keep it moist.

Drain the rice and stir in the black pepper, lemon rind and herbs. Serve the herb rice with the salmon and garnish with lemon slices and herbs.

Chinese mackerel fillets

Serves 4

   10 ml (2 tsp) olive oil
   2 carrots, peeled and thinly sliced
   2.5 cm (1 inch) piece of fresh root ginger, peeled and finely
      sliced
   4 spring onions, trimmed and sliced
   2 x 350–450 g (12 oz–1 lb) mackerel, filleted
   225 g (8 oz) can water chestnuts, drained and sliced
   15 ml (1 tbsp) lemon juice
   15 ml (1 tbsp) light soy sauce
   freshly ground pepper
   spring onions, to garnish

Heat the oil in a large pan and cook the carrots, ginger and
onions for 2 minutes. Add the mackerel fillets and cook for a
further 2 minutes. Turn the fillets over, then add the water
chestnuts, lemon juice and soy sauce. Cook for 3–4
minutes, then season with black pepper. Garnish with
spring onions.

Spicy Jamaican fish

Serves 2

   2 x 375 g (13 oz) whole mackerel, cleaned
   salt and freshly ground pepper
   4 spring onions, trimmed and finely chopped
   15 g (½ oz) red or green chillies, finely chopped (optional)
   1 clove garlic, skinned and crushed
   pinch of dried oregano
   10 ml (2 tsp) lemon juice
   15 ml (1 tbsp) olive oil
   1 small onion, skinned and chopped
   400 g (14 oz) can chopped tomatoes
   15 ml (1 tbsp) hot chilli sauce
   15 ml (1 tbsp) cornflour (optional)

Make three diagonal cuts on one side of the fish (the head can be removed if preferred). Season the fish. Mix the onions, chillies, if using, garlic, oregano and lemon juice together and press into the slits of the fish. Leave to marinate in the refrigerator for about 1 hour.

Heat the oil in a large pan and fry the onion until soft. Mix in the tomatoes, chilli sauce and seasoning. Lay the fish on top of the mixture. Cover and cook over a gentle heat for 20–25 minutes. Remove the fish from the pan and serve with the sauce, thickened with cornflour, if liked.

Orange-stuffed mackerel

Serves 4

> 30 g (1 oz) polyunsaturated margarine
> 1 onion, skinned and chopped
> 60 g (2 oz) long grain rice, cooked
> 30 g (1 oz) walnuts, chopped
> 30 g (1 oz) seedless raisins
> grated rind and juice of 3 medium oranges
> salt and freshly ground pepper
> 4 mackerel, about 300 g (10 oz) each, cleaned and boned, heads
>   and tails removed
> 2 egg yolks
> 5 ml (1 tsp) cornflour
> 30 ml (2 tbsp) white wine
> parsley sprigs, to garnish

Melt the margarine in a heavy-based frying pan and cook the onion until soft. Stir in the cooked rice, walnuts, raisins and orange rind. Season. Stuff the fish with orange mixture, then wrap in greased foil. Bake in a preheated oven at 180°C (350°F) mark 4 for 25–30 minutes or until the fish is tender.

Meanwhile, beat the egg yolks and cornflour together in a pan and stir in the orange juice and wine. Cook gently, stirring, until the sauce thickens. Do not boil. Unwrap the fish, then place on a warmed serving dish. Pour the sauce over and garnish with parsley sprigs.

Spaghetti with anchovy and oregano sauce

Serves 4

100 ml (3½ fl oz) olive oil
2 cloves garlic
60 g (2 oz) canned anchovy fillets, drained
450 g (1 lb) spaghetti
10 ml (2 tsp) finely chopped fresh oregano
salt and freshly ground pepper
45 ml (3 tbsp) chopped fresh parsley
grated Parmesan cheese, to serve

Heat the oil in a small saucepan and fry the garlic until golden. Reduce the heat to very low, stir in the anchovies and cook gently until the anchovies have completely disintegrated.

Meanwhile, cook the spaghetti in plenty of boiling salted water until cooked. Stir the oregano and black pepper into the sauce. Drain the spaghetti well and turn into a warmed serving dish. Pour over the sauce, sprinkle with the parsley and gently toss together. Serve with Parmesan cheese and a side salad.

Halibut with wine and tomatoes

Serves 6

30 ml (2 tbsp) olive oil
175 g (6 oz) onion, skinned and finely chopped
15 g (½ oz) fresh root ginger, peeled and finely chopped
45 ml (3 tbsp) plain flour
150 ml (¼ pint) medium dry white wine
450 g (1 lb) tomatoes, skinned and roughly chopped
175 g (6 oz) mushrooms, quartered
15 ml (1 tbsp) tomato purée
salt and freshly ground pepper
3 large or 6 small halibut or cod steaks, about 1 kg (2 lb) total
    weight

Heat the oil in a frying pan and cook the onion and ginger over a gentle heat for about 5 minutes, stirring occasionally. Stir in 30 ml (2 tbsp) of the flour, then the wine, tomatoes, mushrooms, tomato purée and seasoning. Bring to the boil and cook for 2 minutes. Remove from the heat and cool slightly.

Meanwhile, skin the steaks. Coat with the remaining flour and place in a shallow ovenproof dish, which will take the fish in a single layer. Spoon over the tomato sauce. Cover the dish tightly and bake in a preheated oven at 180°C (350°F) mark 4 for about 30 minutes or until the fish eases away from the bone when tested with a sharp knife.

Salmon croquettes

Canned tuna may be used in place of salmon.

Serves 3

    30 g (1 oz) polyunsaturated margarine
    1 small onion, skinned and chopped
    30 ml (2 tbsp) plain flour
    120 ml (4 fl oz) skimmed milk
    194 g (7¾ oz) can pink salmon, drained
    freshly ground pepper
    60 ml (4 tbsp) breadcrumbs
    30 ml (2 tbsp) olive oil

Melt the margarine in a pan and fry the onion until soft but not browned. Stir in the flour and cook for 1 minute, stirring continuously. Slowly pour in the milk and cook until thickened, stirring all the time. Stir in the salmon, pepper and half the breadcrumbs. Mix thoroughly and shape into six croquettes. Coat with the remaining breadcrumbs. Heat the olive oil in a frying pan and fry the croquettes until evenly brown. Drain on absorbent kitchen paper.

Savoury halibut

Serves 4

4 halibut steaks
salt and freshly ground pepper
50 ml (2 fl oz) olive oil
15 ml (1 tbsp) lemon juice
30 ml (2 tbsp) chopped fresh parsley and chives
lemon slices, to garnish

Sprinkle the fish with seasoning to taste. Place the fish in a grill pan and pour the oil over the fish. Cook under a preheated moderate grill for about 12–15 minutes, depending on thickness, turning once. Transfer the fish to a warmed serving dish.

Pour the contents of the grill pan into a saucepan and add the lemon juice and herbs. Heat but do not boil, stirring continuously, then pour over the fish. Garnish with lemon slices and serve with new potatoes and vegetables.

9

White Fish Main Meals

Potato-topped fish pie

Serves 4

> 450 g (1 lb) celeriac, peeled and cut into chunks
> 700 g (1½ lb) potatoes, peeled and cut into chunks
> salt and freshly ground pepper
> 700 g (1½ lb) whiting, cod or haddock fillet
> 150 ml (¼ pint) semi-skimmed milk
> bay leaves and peppercorns, for flavouring
> 30 g (1 oz) polyunsaturated margarine
> 125 g (4 oz) courgettes, trimmed and thinly sliced
> 30 ml (2 tbsp) plain flour
> 90 g (3 oz) button mushrooms, halved
> 45 ml (3 tbsp) Greek strained yogurt

Boil the celeriac and potatoes together in a saucepan of salted water until tender. Drain. Place the fish in a sauté pan, pour over the milk and 150 ml (¼ pint) water. Add bay leaves and peppercorns, cover and poach for about 10 minutes or until just tender. Using a fish slice, remove the fish from the pan and flake into large pieces, discarding any skin and bones. Strain the liquor into a jug and reserve.

Rinse the sauté pan, add the margarine and cook the courgettes for 1–2 minutes. Mix in the flour and cook for a further 2–3 minutes. Stir in the reserved liquor, bring to the boil and boil for 1–2 minutes or until thickened. Add the mushrooms and fish and adjust seasoning. Pour into a 1.6 litre (2¾ pint) pie dish.

Mash the celeriac and potatoes until smooth. Beat in the yogurt, then season to taste. Spread on top of the fish. Place the dish on a baking sheet. Bake in a preheated oven at 200°C (400°F) mark 6 for about 25 minutes.

Paupiettes of plaice

Serves 2

1 large plaice or lemon sole, filleted
a little polyunsaturated margarine
125 g (4 oz) mushrooms, thinly sliced
15 ml (1 tbsp) olive oil
1 small onion, skinned and chopped
1 tomato, skinned and chopped
salt and freshly ground pepper
chopped fresh parsley, to garnish

Lightly grease a large sheet of foil with polyunsaturated margarine and arrange two fillets in the shape of the fish on the foil. Put half the mushrooms down the centre of the fish. Heat the oil in a pan and fry the onion and tomato until soft, then drain and add to the mushrooms. Add another layer of mushrooms and sandwich together with the remaining fillets. Season. Fold the foil over to seal in the juices and place in an ovenproof dish. Cook in a preheated oven at 150°C (300°F) mark 2 for about 15–20 minutes. Serve garnished with chopped parsley.

Neptune pie

Serves 4

1 kg (2 lb) coley fillets, skinned and cubed
salt and freshly ground pepper
200 g (7 oz) can sweetcorn, drained
225 g (8 oz) tomatoes, sliced
225 g (8 oz) potatoes, peeled and parboiled
60 g (2 oz) Cheddar cheese, grated

Place the fish in an ovenproof dish and season well. Sprinkle with the sweetcorn and cover with the tomatoes. Thinly slice the potatoes and place over the fish mixture, partially covering the tomato. Sprinkle with the cheese. Bake in a preheated oven at 190°C (375°F) mark 5 for about 20 minutes until the cheese is golden brown.

French-style sole with tomatoes

Serves 4

    450 g (1 lb) tomatoes, skinned, seeded and chopped
    30 ml (2 tbsp) shallots, skinned and finely chopped
    30 ml (2 tbsp) finely chopped fresh parsley
    2.5 ml (½ tsp) salt
    freshly ground pepper
    700 g (1½ lb) sole fillets
    175 ml (6 fl oz) dry white wine
    30 ml (2 tbsp) polyunsaturated margarine
    30 ml (2 tbsp) flour
    2.5 ml (½ tsp) sugar
    45–60 ml (3–4 tbsp) natural yogurt

Mix the tomatoes, shallots, parsley and seasoning together; place in the bottom of an oiled, flat, flameproof baking dish. Place the fillets over the tomato mixture. Add the wine and 50 ml (2 fl oz) water and bring to simmering point on top of the cooker. Cover and cook in a preheated oven at 170°C (325°F) mark 3 for 13–15 minutes until the fish is cooked. Transfer the fish to a serving dish and keep warm.

Boil the juices until reduced to about half. Mix the margarine and flour together. Stir into the juices and cook until thickened. Add the sugar, yogurt and any juices drained from the fish on the serving dish. Pour over the fish and serve.

Prawn Provençale

Serves 4

    30 ml (2 tbsp) olive oil
    1 onion, skinned and chopped
    1 clove garlic, skinned and crushed
    125 g (4 oz) button mushrooms, sliced
    400 g (14 oz) can chopped tomatoes
    150 ml (¼ pint) dry white wine
    salt and freshly ground pepper
    10 ml (2 tsp) tomato purée
    pinch of dried mixed herbs
    15 ml (1 tbsp) cornflour
    450 g (1 lb) peeled prawns (defrosted if frozen)

Heat the oil in a pan and fry the onion, garlic and mushrooms until soft. Add the tomatoes, wine, seasoning, tomato purée and herbs and simmer gently for 10 minutes. Blend the cornflour with a little water and add to the mixture with the prawns. Stir continuously until thickened and simmer for a further 4–5 minutes. Serve on a bed of pasta or rice with a salad.

Plaki

This dish can be found in Greece and throughout the Middle East. Whole sea bass is an ideal choice, but halibut, grey mullet, sea bream, cod, John Dory or haddock are all good alternatives.

Serves 4

    1 kg (2 lb) fish, left whole or cut into thick steaks
    juice of 1 lemon
    60 ml (4 tbsp) olive oil
    2 large onions, skinned and thinly sliced
    3 cloves garlic, skinned and crushed
    400 g (14 oz) can tomatoes, drained and finely chopped
    175 ml (6 fl oz) dry white wine
    15 ml (1 tbsp) dried oregano
    1 bay leaf
    salt and freshly ground pepper
    75 ml (5 tbsp) chopped fresh parsley

Place the fish in a baking dish and pour the lemon juice over it. If using a whole fish, pour some of the juice inside it. Heat the oil in a frying pan and fry the onions and garlic until golden. Add the tomatoes, breaking them up with a fork, and cook for a further 5 minutes. Add the wine, oregano, bay leaf and seasoning. Bring to the boil, remove from the heat, add the parsley and cool for 5 minutes. Pour the sauce over the fish. Bake uncovered in a preheated oven at 180°C (350°F) mark 4 for 40 minutes. Serve accompanied by hot crusty bread.

Savoury fish steaks

Serves 4

4 x 175–225 g (6–8 oz) cod steaks
salt and freshly ground pepper
45 ml (3 tbsp) lemon juice
30 ml (2 tbsp) polyunsaturated margarine
15 ml (1 tbsp) wholegrain mustard or 15 ml (1 tbsp) tomato
   purée

Place the cod steaks on a foil-lined grill tray. Season and sprinkle with the lemon juice. Mix the margarine with the mustard or tomato purée and spread over the fish steaks. Cook under a preheated medium grill for 7–10 minutes until the fish is cooked. Serve hot with a selection of vegetables.

Whiting with courgettes and rosemary

Serves 4

4 x 125–175 g (4–6 oz) whiting fillets, skinned
30 g (1 oz) wholemeal flour
salt and freshly ground pepper
30 g (1 oz) polyunsaturated margarine
2 small courgettes, trimmed and cut into sticks
30 ml (2 tbsp) lemon juice
5 ml (1 tsp) dried rosemary and lemon slices, to garnish

Cut each fillet in four, removing any small bones. Dust with seasoned flour. Melt the margarine in a large frying pan and gently cook the fillets for 2 minutes. Turn the fillets, add the courgettes and lemon juice. Cover and simmer for 5–6 minutes. Transfer to warmed serving dish and garnish with rosemary and lemon slices.

Lemon sole with almonds and bananas

Serves 4

    4 x 175 g (6 oz) lemon sole fillets, skinned
    30 g (1 oz) polyunsaturated margarine
    2 bananas, sliced
    30 g (1 oz) flaked almonds
    45 ml (3 tbsp) lemon juice
    salt and freshly ground pepper
    parsley, to garnish

Fold the fillets in half. Melt the margarine in a pan and cook the fillets for 5–6 minutes, turning once. Add the bananas, almonds, lemon juice and seasoning. Cover and cook for a further 3–4 minutes. Garnish with parsley.

Fish casserole

Serves 4

    125 g (4 oz) mushrooms, chopped
    20 ml (4 tsp) breadcrumbs
    5 ml (1 tsp) grated lemon rind
    175 g (6 oz) tomatoes, skinned and chopped
    salt and freshly ground pepper
    4 medium plaice fillets, skinned
    150 ml (¼ pint) dry white wine

Mix together 50 g (2 oz) of the mushrooms, the bread-crumbs, lemon rind, tomatoes and seasoning. Place equal amounts of the mixture on the fish fillets, roll up and place in a casserole. Cover the plaice with the remaining mushrooms. Pour the wine over the fish. Cover and cook in a preheated oven at 190°C (375°F) mark 5 for 20–25 minutes.

Crispy orange cod

Serves 4

4 slices of brown bread
45 g (1½ oz) polyunsaturated margarine
1 clove garlic, skinned and crushed
grated rind and juice of 1 orange
4 cod fillets
salt and freshly ground pepper

Place the bread in a blender to make crumbs. Melt the margarine in a frying pan and stir in the breadcrumbs. Add the garlic and orange rind. Place the fish in an oiled oven-proof dish and cover with the orange and breadcrumb mixture. Season and add the orange juice. Bake in a pre-heated oven at 190°C (375°F) mark 5 for 25–30 minutes. Serve with new potatoes and green salad.

Cod with mushrooms

Serves 4

4 pieces of cod fillet, skinned
salt and freshly ground pepper
30 g (1 oz) plain flour
60 ml (4 tbsp) olive oil
1 medium onion, skinned and chopped
125 g (4 oz) mushrooms, sliced
skimmed milk
chopped fresh parsley

Sprinkle the cod with seasoning and coat in flour. Put a sheet of foil on a baking tin and coat the centre with a little oil. Place the cod pieces on the foil. Heat the remainder of the oil (about 30 ml/2 tbsp) in a pan and cook the onion and mushrooms until just soft but not browned. Pour over the fish and fold the foil over to enclose the fish. Cook in a preheated oven at 190°C (375°F) mark 5 for 35–40 minutes.

Drain the juices into a measuring jug and add sufficient milk to make up to 300 ml (½ pint). Boil for 1 minute, stirring continuously. Season to taste and add the parsley. Pour the sauce over the fish and serve.

Baked fish steaks

Serves 4

>700 g (1½ lb) white fish steaks
>30 ml (2 tbsp) olive oil
>salt and freshly ground pepper
>chopped fresh parsley, to garnish
>lemon slices, to serve

Place the fish on a preheated oiled baking tin. Add the olive oil and sprinkle with seasoning. Bake in a preheated oven at 240°C (475°F) mark 9 until the fish flakes easily. Garnish with chopped parsley and serve with new potatoes, petits pois and a slice of lemon.

Spicy coley

Serves 4–6

>1 kg (2 lb) coley fillets, skinned
>300 ml (½ pint) tomato juice
>60 ml (4 tbsp) French dressing
>pinch of cayenne pepper or dash of Tabasco sauce (optional)

Cut the fish into portions and place in a shallow dish. Combine the remaining ingredients, pour over the fish and allow to stand for 30 minutes, turning once. Remove the fish and place on a lightly oiled grill pan, reserving the sauce for basting. Cook under a preheated grill for 4–5 minutes. Turn carefully, baste with the sauce and grill for another 4–5 minutes. Serve hot with baked jacket potatoes and mixed vegetables.

10

Microwave Fish Recipes

Microwaving is now regarded as one of the very best methods of cooking fish as it maintains its texture, moisture and appearance. The microwave is ideal for defrosting and cooking all types of fish. You can use it to fry fish lightly in a browning dish as well as for poaching, steaming and baking. In many of these recipes, the skin is removed from the fish before cooking but, if not, it is important to slit the skin of whole fish in two or three places to prevent bursting. Cover the fish during cooking. Fish cooks very quickly in the microwave, so undercook and allow for standing time.

Defrosting frozen fish

All fish can be successfully defrosted quickly by using the defrost setting on your microwave oven. Remember fish defrosts so quickly that care must be taken to ensure that it does not cook. The following points are guidelines to defrosting fish:

- Arrange the fish in a single layer in a shallow dish, in order to collect any excess liquid.
- Avoid overloading the dish as this prolongs defrosting time.
- To help prevent the fish drying out during defrosting, cover the container and turn the fish over once.
- To defrost fish in the microwave, use an average of 5 minutes per 450 g (1 lb) on the DEFROST power level.
- To prevent uneven defrosting or cooking, arrange the thickest part of the fish towards the edge of the dish and fold tail pieces underneath.

- The defrosting time will vary according to the thickness of the fish; thin fillets will defrost much quicker than thick ones.
- Allow a 'standing time' equal to that of defrosting to ensure even results.

Reheating of cooked fish dishes

To reheat a cooked fish dish, set the power control to HIGH and microwave for the minimum amount of time in order to prevent overcooking.

Allow a 3-minute standing time immediately prior to serving so that the heat can disperse throughout the fish.

If the fish dish is frozen, defrost before reheating.

The following recipes are suitable for use in microwave ovens with 600–700 watt output. For use in 500 watt microwave ovens, increase the cooking times by 10–15 seconds per minute.

Garlic prawns and scallops

Serves 2

> 15 g (½ oz) polyunsaturated margarine
> 1 clove garlic, skinned and crushed
> 1 small onion, skinned and finely chopped
> 2 scallops, sliced
> 225 g (8 oz) peeled prawns
> salt and freshly ground pepper
> 15 ml (1 tbsp) fromage frais

Place the margarine in a heatpoof dish and microwave on HIGH for 30 seconds. Stir in the garlic and onion and microwave on HIGH for a further ½–1 minute. Stir in the scallops and prawns, cover and microwave on HIGH for 1½–2½ minutes, stirring after 1 minute. Leave to stand, covered, for 1 minute. Season and spoon over the 15 ml (1 tbsp) fromage frais. Serve with French bread.

Sweet and sour haddock

Serves 4

450 g (1 lb) haddock fillet, skinned and cubed
225 g (8 oz) can pineapple pieces in natural juice
½ bunch spring onions, trimmed and chopped

For the sauce

juice from canned pineapple
15 ml (1 tbsp) sugar
30 ml (2 tbsp) soy sauce
30 ml (2 tbsp) tomato ketchup
15 ml (1 tbsp) cornflour
salt and freshly ground pepper

Place the fish in a heatproof dish and mix in the drained pineapple pieces and onions. Pour the reserved pineapple juice into a measuring jug and make up to 300 ml (½ pint) with water. Add the remaining sauce ingredients, except seasoning. Stir well. Microwave, uncovered, on HIGH for 2–3 minutes, stirring every minute. Pour the hot sauce over the fish mixture, cover and microwave on HIGH for 2½–3½ minutes, stirring once. Leave to stand, covered, for 2 minutes. Season to taste. Serve with brown rice or noodles and a crispy green salad.

Tangy cod steaks

Serves 3

3 x 175 g (6–8 oz) cod steaks, fresh or defrosted
10 ml (2 tsp) lemon juice
1 small onion, skinned and chopped
10 ml (2 tsp) olive oil
10 ml (2 tsp) plain flour
120 ml (4 fl oz) fish or chicken stock
10 ml (2 tsp) tomato purée
10 ml (2 tsp) Worcestershire sauce
10 ml (2 tsp) vinegar
10 ml (2 tsp) brown sugar
salt and freshly ground pepper

Arrange the cod steaks in a shallow heatproof dish. Sprinkle over the lemon juice. Cover and microwave on HIGH for 3–4 minutes or until cooked. Leave to stand, still covered.

Place the onion and oil in a bowl, cover and microwave on HIGH for 2 minutes. Stir in the flour and microwave on HIGH for 30 seconds. Add the remaining ingredients, except the fish and seasoning, stirring well. Microwave the sauce on HIGH for 1 minute, stirring halfway. Season to taste.

Arrange the cod steaks on a warmed serving dish and pour over the sauce. Serve immediately with a selection of vegetables.

Seafood jackets

Serves 4

    4 x 225 g (8 oz) baking potatoes
    60 g (2 oz) mushrooms, thinly sliced
    225 g (8 oz) white fish fillets, skinned and thinly sliced
    salt and freshly ground pepper
    60 g (2 oz) Leicester cheese, finely grated

Prick the potatoes well and microwave on HIGH for about 15 minutes or until cooked. Leave to stand while preparing the filling. Place the mushrooms in a small bowl and microwave on HIGH for 2 minutes. Drain.

Slice a 'lid' horizontally off the potatoes and scoop out most of the centres into a large bowl. Add the mushrooms, fish, seasoning and two-thirds of the cheese. Mix well together. Pile the mixture into the potato cases and sprinkle over the remaining cheese. Microwave on HIGH for 3–4 minutes. Leave to stand for 2 minutes before serving.

Fish Waldorf

Serves 6

> 450 g (1 lb) white fish fillets, skinned and cubed
> lemon juice
> ½ crisp lettuce, shredded
> 2 red apples, cored and sliced
> 60 ml (4 tbsp) natural yogurt
> 60 ml (4 tbsp) mayonnaise
> 60 g (2 oz) walnuts, chopped .
> 60 g (2 oz) seedless grapes, halved
> 2 sticks of celery, diced
> salt and freshly ground pepper

Place the fish in a shallow heatproof dish and sprinkle with a little lemon juice. Loosely cover and microwave on HIGH for 2–3 minutes. Leave to stand for 2 minutes. Drain, cool and refrigerate.

In a large bowl, mix together the fish and remaining ingredients. Season to taste. Serve with wholemeal rolls.

Skate with oranges

Serves 4

> 550 g (1¼ lb) skinned skate wings, cut into 4 pieces
> polyunsaturated margarine or olive oil, for greasing
> 1 large orange, peeled and thinly sliced
> 3 spring onions, trimmed and chopped, or 1 small onion,
>   skinned and finely chopped
> 10 ml (2 tsp) soy sauce
> salt and freshly ground pepper

Arrange the skate wings in a lightly greased heatproof dish so that the thick and thin parts overlap. Top with the orange slices. Put the onion into a small bowl with the soy sauce. Cover and microwave on HIGH for ½–1 minute or until beginning to soften. Pour over the fish, cover and microwave on HIGH for 6–8 minutes. Leave to stand, covered, for 2 minutes. Season before serving with boiled new potatoes and peas.

Poached salmon

Serves 2

1 glass dry white wine (a small can of wine may be used)
6 black peppercorns
1 lemon, sliced
1 bay leaf
2 x 175 g (6 oz) salmon steaks

Place the wine, a glass of water, peppercorns, lemon and bay leaf in a glass dish. Add the salmon steaks, cover and microwave on HIGH for 1 minute. Turn the salmon and microwave on HIGH for a further 1 minute. Allow the salmon to cool, then serve with new potatoes and salad.

Herring salad

Serves 2

60 g (2 oz) low-fat cottage cheese with chives or onion and
    peppers
2 medium herring, filleted and skinned

Spoon equal amounts of cottage cheese on the head end of each fillet, flesh side up, then roll up from head to tail. Place in a heatproof dish. Cover and microwave on DEFROST for 5–6 minutes or until the herring is cooked. Leave to stand for 2 minutes before draining. Chill. Serve with a green salad.

Citrus fish

Serves 1

1 small courgette, cut into matchsticks
1 orange, peeled and segmented
pinch of dried rosemary
salt and freshly ground pepper
225 g (8 oz) white fish fillet, fresh or defrosted, skinned
5 ml (1 tsp) lemon juice

Place the courgette and orange segments in a heatproof dish. Sprinkle over half of the rosemary and add the seasoning. Roll the fillet from head to tail, skinned side uppermost and arrange on top of the courgettes and oranges. Spoon over the lemon juice and remaining rosemary. Cover and microwave on HIGH for 2–3 minutes or until the fish is cooked. Leave to stand for 2 minutes before serving. Serve with boiled new potatoes and a selection of vegetables.

Paper-wrapped lemon fillet

Serves 2

    15 g (½ oz) polyunsaturated margarine
    ½ small onion, skinned and finely chopped
    5 ml (1 tsp) dried parsley (optional)
    2.5 ml (½ tsp) dried mixed herbs
    grated rind of ½ lemon
    10 ml (2 tsp) lemon juice
    90 ml (6 tsp) wholemeal breadcrumbs
    2 pinches of ground ginger
    salt and freshly ground pepper
    2 x 175–225 g (6–8 oz) lemon sole fillets, skinned

Cut two pieces of greaseproof paper 20 x 25 cm (8 x 10 inches). Place the margarine in a bowl and microwave on HIGH for 30 seconds. Use a little margarine to grease the centres of the greaseproof paper. Add the onion to the remaining margarine, cover and microwave on HIGH for 1–2 minutes.

Stir in the parsley, herbs, lemon rind and juice, and breadcrumbs. Sprinkle the prepared greaseproof paper with a little ginger and seasoning. Place the fish fillets, skinned side uppermost, on the greaseproof paper and cover half the fish with the breadcrumb mixture. Fold the fillet over and wrap in paper by twisting the edges together, leaving a small gap at one corner for steam to escape. Arrange the parcels on a heatproof plate and microwave on HIGH for 2–2½ minutes. Leave to stand for 1 minute. Serve in the wraps with stir-fried vegetables and rice.

Fish Florentine

Serves 2

  125 g (4 oz) frozen leaf spinach, defrosted and drained
  225 g (8 oz) white fish fillets, fresh or defrosted, skinned and
    cubed
  10 ml (2 tsp) cornflour
  150 ml (¼ pint) semi-skimmed milk
  30 g (1 oz) Leicester cheese, finely grated
  salt and freshly ground pepper

Place the spinach in the base of a shallow heatproof dish.
Cover and microwave on HIGH for 1 minute until heated
through. Spoon the fish over the spinach. Blend the
cornflour with the milk in a bowl. Microwave on HIGH for
1–2 minutes, whisking every minute until the sauce thickens. Add two-thirds of the cheese to the sauce, season to
taste and pour over the fish. Sprinkle the remaining cheese
on top. Microwave on HIGH for 2 minutes. Leave to stand
for 2 minutes. Serve with a crunchy mixed salad.

Tomato whiting

Serves 2

  15 ml (1 tbsp) olive oil
  1 small onion, skinned and finely chopped
  200 g (7 oz) can chopped tomatoes
  2.5 ml (½ tsp) dried mixed herbs
  350 g (12 oz) whiting fillets, skinned
  salt and freshly ground pepper

Place the oil in a shallow ovenproof dish and microwave on
HIGH for 30 seconds. Stir in the onion, cover and microwave
on HIGH for 2–3 minutes or until soft. Pour in the tomatoes
and stir in the herbs. Divide the whiting into two portions
and add to the tomato mixture. Cover and microwave on
HIGH for 2½–3 minutes. Leave to stand, covered, for 1
minute. Season before serving with brown rice and
vegetables.

Crunchy-topped coley

Serves 1

175 g (6 oz) thick coley fillet, skinned
5 ml (1 tsp) lemon juice
1 medium flat mushroom, finely chopped
5 ml (1 tsp) polyunsaturated margarine
30 ml (2 tbsp) cornflakes or fresh breadcrumbs
5 ml (1 tsp) wholegrain or French mustard
pinch of dried parsley (optional)
salt and freshly ground pepper

Place the coley fillet in a shallow ovenproof dish. Sprinkle with the lemon juice and mushroom. Dot with the margarine. Cover and microwave on HIGH for 1½–2 minutes. Meanwhile, mix together the cornflakes or breadcrumbs, mustard, parsley, if using, and seasoning. Spoon evenly over the fish and microwave, uncovered, on HIGH for ½–1 minute. Leave to stand for 30 seconds. Serve with a baked jacket potato and sweetcorn.

Welsh cod bake

Serves 4

15 ml (1 tbsp) olive oil
2–3 leeks, trimmed, washed and thinly sliced
450 g (1 lb) cod fillet, skinned and cubed
10 ml (2 tsp) lemon juice
60 g (2 oz) walnuts, hazelnuts or almonds, roughly chopped
15 ml (1 tbsp) chopped fresh parsley (optional)
salt and freshly ground pepper

Place the oil in a shallow heatproof dish and microwave on HIGH for 30 seconds. Stir in the leeks, cover and microwave on HIGH for 1½–2 minutes. Stir in the fish, lemon juice, nuts and parsley, if used. Cover and microwave on HIGH for 2½–3 minutes. Leave to stand, covered, for 2 minutes. Season and serve with baked jacket potatoes and vegetables.

Fish and pasta Creole

Serves 4

1 clove garlic, skinned and crushed
2–3 sticks of celery, sliced
300 ml (½ pint) chicken stock or boiling water
400 g (14 oz) can chopped tomatoes
15 ml (1 tbsp) tomato purée
125 g (4 oz) wholewheat pasta
1 bay leaf
175 g (6 oz) can sweetcorn, drained
700 g (1½ lb) monkfish tails, filleted, skinned and cubed
salt and freshly ground pepper
chopped fresh parsley, to garnish

Put the garlic, celery and stock in a casserole, cover and microwave on HIGH for 5 minutes. Stir in the tomatoes, tomato purée, pasta and bay leaf. Cover and microwave on HIGH for 2 minutes. Stir in the sweetcorn and fish, cover and microwave on HIGH for 2 minutes.

Remove the bay leaf, season well and sprinkle with the chopped parsley before serving.

Fruity stuffed mackerel

Serves 4

1 apple, cored and chopped
60 g (2 oz) sultanas
5 ml (1 tsp) chopped fresh tarragon
30 ml (2 tbsp) lemon juice
15 g (½ oz) polyunsaturated margarine
60 g (2 oz) porridge oats
salt and freshly ground pepper
4 x 225–300 g (8–10 oz) mackerel fillets

Place the apple, sultanas, tarragon, lemon juice and margarine in a bowl. Cover and microwave on HIGH for 2 minutes until the apple has softened a little. Stir in the oats and seasoning.

Divide the filling into four. Place the mackerel on a board, skin side down. Spread the filling over the mackerel and roll up the fish from the head ends. Secure the rolls with wooden cocktail sticks and place in a shallow heatproof dish. Cover and microwave on HIGH for 4 minutes. Allow to stand, covered, for 2 minutes.

Mediterranean-style halibut

Serves 4

    1 aubergine, sliced
    salt
    1 onion, skinned and sliced
    1 small green pepper, seeded and sliced
    15 ml (1 tbsp) olive oil
    60 g (2 oz) button mushrooms, sliced
    1 clove garlic, skinned and crushed
    225 g (8 oz) can tomatoes
    5 ml (1 tsp) marjoram
    6 stoned black olives
    15 ml (1 tbsp) tomato purée
    freshly ground pepper
    2 x 350 g (12 oz) halibut steaks

Sprinkle the aubergine slices with salt and leave for 30 minutes. Drain and rinse. Place the onion, green pepper and oil in a casserole. Cover and microwave on HIGH for 3 minutes. Stir in the aubergine, mushrooms and garlic, cover and microwave on HIGH for 3 minutes. Stir in the tomatoes, half the marjoram, the olives and tomato purée. Microwave on HIGH, uncovered, for 10 minutes, stirring twice to break up the tomatoes. Season, then place the halibut on top. Cover and microwave on HIGH for 6–7 minutes. Leave to stand, covered, for 3 minutes before serving. Garnish with the remaining marjoram.

Oriental sea bass

Serves 4

1 sea bass, weighing about 1.1–1.4 kg (2½–3 lb)
15 ml (1 tbsp) olive oil
4 spring onions, trimmed and sliced
60 ml (4 tbsp) dark soy sauce
15 ml (1 tbsp) sesame oil
2 cloves garlic, skinned and crushed
30 ml (2 tbsp) sesame seeds
8 water chestnuts, sliced
1 carrot, peeled and sliced
bamboo shoots and spring onion tassels, to garnish

Ask the fishmonger to clean and scale the fish for you and remove the head. Wash and dry the fish. Trim the tail and protect with foil. Brush a sheet of baking parchment, large enough to enclose the whole fish, with the olive oil. Lay the fish on the paper and sprinkle over the spring onions, soy sauce, sesame oil, garlic, sesame seeds, water chestnuts and carrot. Wrap and enclose the fish, twisting the edges to seal the parcel. Microwave on HIGH for 10–14 minutes. Leave to stand, without unwrapping, for 5 minutes. Remove from the paper and place on a warmed serving dish. Garnish with oriental vegetables.

Skate with wine and fennel

Serves 4

700 g (1½ lb) skate wings
60 ml (2 fl oz) dry white wine
10 ml (2 tsp) chopped fennel leaves
60 g (2 oz) mange tout
½ melon, peeled, seeded and cut into balls
fennel sprigs, to garnish

Place the skate wings in a shallow heatproof dish in a single layer. Pour over the wine and add the fennel. Cover and microwave on HIGH for 6–8 minutes. Leave to stand, covered, for 2 minutes. Transfer to a serving dish and keep covered. Add the mange tout to the cooking juices, cover and microwave on HIGH for 1 minute. Stir in the melon balls and microwave on HIGH for a further 1 minute. Transfer the mange tout and melon balls to the serving dish and spoon the juices over the fish. Garnish with fennel sprigs.

Salmon steaks with cucumber sauce

Serves 4

>   4 x 175 g (6 oz) salmon steaks, 2.5 cm (1 inch) thick
>   12 slices of cucumber
>   60 ml (4 tbsp) dry white wine or fish stock
>   ½ small cucumber, grated
>   30 g (1 oz) polyunsaturated margarine
>   30 ml (2 tbsp) chopped dill
>   4 spring onions, trimmed and finely chopped
>   60 ml (4 tbsp) natural yogurt
>   30 ml (2 tbsp) low-calorie mayonnaise
>   salt and freshly ground pepper

Place the salmon steaks in a shallow dish and arrange three slices of cucumber on each steak. Pour over the wine or stock and cover.

For the sauce, squeeze the excess liquid out of the grated cucumber and place in a bowl with the margarine. Cover and microwave on HIGH for 4 minutes. Leave to cool.

Microwave the salmon on HIGH for 6–7 minutes or until cooked. Leave to stand for 2 minutes.

Meanwhile, mix together the cooked cucumber, dill, spring onions, yogurt and mayonnaise. Season to taste. Chill until required. Serve the salmon with the sauce, a mixed salad and boiled new potatoes.

11

Fish Meals for Special Occasions

It has been our policy in the Eskimo diet to avoid extremes. Without the occasional treat, life would be unhappy and we are all for increasing the happiness factor in our lives. In this section we allow much larger amounts of saturated fat in the meals on the basis that such meals will be 'occasional' in both senses of the word.

STARTERS

Prawns Newburg

Serve on a large bread croustade as a starter, or on a bed of rice as a main course, with fresh watercress.

Serves 4

    4 x 2 cm (¾ inch) thick slices of white bread, crusts removed
    60 g (2 oz) polyunsaturated margarine
    45 ml (3 tbsp) Madeira
    10 ml (2 tsp) brandy
    350 g (12 oz) peeled prawns
    salt and freshly ground pepper
    2 egg yolks
    150 ml (¼ pint) double cream
    2.5 ml (½ tsp) paprika
    watercress, to serve

Place the slices of bread on a baking tray. Melt half the margarine and brush over the bread. Bake in a preheated oven at 150°C (300°F) mark 2 for 25 minutes. Meanwhile, melt the remaining margarine in a pan and add the Madeira and brandy. Simmer for 5 minutes, then add the prawns. Season and simmer for 2 minutes. Remove from the heat.

Mix the egg yolks with the cream and stir into the pan. Cook over a gentle heat for 5 minutes, stirring, until the sauce thickens. Do not allow the mixture to boil or it will curdle. Spoon the prawns and sauce onto the baked bread and sprinkle with paprika. Serve hot with watercress.

Langoustine soufflés

These individual soufflés can be served as a light, appetizing starter or as a luncheon dish served with a crisp green salad.

Serves 6

> 225 g (8 oz) raw langoustine tails, shelled
> 300 ml (½ pint) fish stock
> 45 g (1½ oz) polyunsaturated margarine
> 2 shallots, skinned and finely chopped
> 30 ml (2 tbsp) plain flour
> 2 egg yolks
> pinch of cayenne
> pinch of grated nutmeg
> 45 ml (3 tbsp) toasted breadcrumbs
> 3 egg whites
> pinch of salt
> whole langoustines, to garnish (optional)

Poach the langoustine tails in the fish stock in a pan for about 2 minutes. Drain and roughly chop. Reserve the fish stock.

Melt the margarine in a pan and fry the shallots until soft. Stir in the flour and cook for 1 minute. Remove from the heat and gradually stir in the fish stock. Cook, stirring, until the sauce has thickened. Simmer for 1 minute, then remove from the heat and beat in the egg yolks. Stir in the langoustine tails and season well.

Grease six individual 175–200 ml (6–7 fl oz) ramekins and coat the insides with the toasted breadcrumbs. Chill.

Whisk the egg whites with the salt until stiff, then fold them into the sauce. Spoon into the prepared ramekins.

Arrange on a preheated baking sheet. Bake in a preheated oven at 180°C (350°F) mark 4 for about 20 minutes or until risen and golden. Serve immediately, garnished with langoustines, if liked.

Crab and shrimp bisque

Serves 4–6

30 g (1 oz) polyunsaturated margarine
1 small onion, skinned and finely chopped
1 small clove garlic, skinned and crushed
1 stick celery, diced
150 ml (¼ pint) dry white wine
600 ml (1 pint) fish stock
1 bouquet garni
1 bay leaf
salt and freshly ground pepper
225 g (8 oz) shrimps, peeled
700 g (1½ lb) brown and white crabmeat
150 ml (¼ pint) single cream
15 ml (1 tbsp) brandy
150 ml (¼ pint) natural yogurt, to garnish

Melt the margarine in a large saucepan and fry the onion, garlic and celery until transparent. Add the wine, stock, bouquet garni, bay leaf and seasoning. Simmer for 5–10 minutes to allow the herbs to infuse. Stir in the shrimps, brown crabmeat and half the white crabmeat and simmer for 10 minutes.

Allow to cool slightly, then purée in a blender. Return to the heat and add the cream, brandy and remaining crabmeat. Before serving, swirl with natural yogurt.

Smoked salmon pâté

Serves 6

  175 g (6 oz) smoked salmon 'off-cuts'
  90 g (3 oz) polyunsaturated margarine, melted
  20 ml (4 tsp) lemon juice
  60 ml (4 tbsp) single cream
  freshly ground pepper
  cucumber slices, to garnish
  150 ml (¼ pint) liquid aspic jelly

Roughly cut up the salmon pieces, reserving a few for garnishing, and place in a blender or food processor. Add the margarine, lemon juice and cream, with pepper to taste. Blend the mixture until smooth. Spoon into a 300 ml (½ pint) dish to within 1 cm (½ inch) of the rim. Chill for 1 hour to set.

Garnish with the reserved pieces of smoked salmon and cucumber slices. Spoon over the aspic jelly, which should be just on the point of setting. Chill for 30 minutes to set the aspic. Leave at room temperature for 30 minutes before serving.

Lobster mousse

Serves 4

  1 cooked lobster, 700 g–1 kg (1½–2 lb), or 225 g (8 oz) lobster
    meat
  15 ml (1 tbsp) powdered gelatine
  300 ml (½ pint) whipping cream
  30 ml (2 tbsp) mayonnaise
  juice of 1 lemon
  freshly ground pepper
  2 egg whites
  strips of lemon or lime peel

Prepare the lobster, if necessary. Beat the lobster meat until smooth (in a food processor if necessary). In a heatproof bowl, mix the gelatine with 45 ml (3 tbsp) water and dissolve over a saucepan of simmering water. Stir the gelatine into the lobster meat. Whip the cream and fold into the lobster with the mayonnaise, lemon juice and black pepper.

Beat the egg whites until stiff and fold into the mousse. Pour the mixture into four wetted moulds. Chill until firm. Unmould and serve garnished with lemon or lime peel.

Note: Use 225 g (8 oz) mixed crabmeat instead of lobster meat to make a crab mousse.

Smoked salmon and trout mousses

A special occasion first course to impress your guests. These mousses, coated in a thin layer of smoked salmon, are made from a rich, well-flavoured salmon and trout mixture.

Serves 6

    450 g (1 lb) salmon trout, cleaned
    300 ml (½ pint) milk
    1 bay leaf and 6 peppercorns, to flavour
    15 ml (1 tbsp) powdered gelatine
    30 g (1 oz) polyunsaturated margarine
    30 ml (2 tbsp) plain flour
    salt and freshly ground pepper
    15 ml (1 tbsp) Dijon mustard
    20 ml (4 tsp) tomato ketchup
    175–225 g (6–8 oz) thinly sliced smoked salmon
    150 ml (¼ pint) double cream
    150 ml (¼ pint) mayonnaise
    30 ml (2 tbsp) lemon juice
    black olives and lemon slices, to garnish

Place the trout with the milk and flavourings in a saucepan and poach for about 20 minutes until tender. Drain, reserving the milk. Discard the head, skin and bones. Flake the flesh.

Dissolve the gelatine in 45 ml (3 tbsp) water in a bowl over a pan of simmering water. Stir briskly.

Melt the margarine in a saucepan, add the flour and cook gently, stirring, for 1–2 minutes. Remove from the heat and gradually blend in the reserved milk. Bring to the boil, stirring constantly, then simmer for 3 minutes until thick and smooth. Season to taste and stir in the soaked gelatine.

Purée the sauce, fish, mustard and ketchup in a blender or food processor until smooth. Allow to cool.

Line six lightly oiled 175 ml (6 fl oz) ramekin dishes with the smoked salmon. Whip the cream until softly stiff. Stir the mayonnaise, lemon juice and cream into the fish mixture. Adjust the seasoning. Spoon the mixture into the dishes, cover and chill to set. Carefully turn out the mousses and garnish with black olives and lemon slices.

MAIN COURSES

Stuffed sea bass braised in white wine

Serves 4

2 fennel bulbs, trimmed and thinly sliced
1 sea bass, about 1 kg (2 lb) cleaned
60 g (2 oz) fresh white breadcrumbs
30 ml (2 tbsp) milk
90 g (3 oz) polyunsaturated margarine
2 shallots, skinned and finely chopped
10 ml (2 tsp) finely chopped fresh parsley
5 ml (1 tsp) finely grated lemon rind
2 egg yolks
salt and freshly ground pepper
150 ml (¼ pint) full-bodied dry white wine
30 ml (2 tbsp) dry white vermouth
50 ml (2 fl oz) double cream
fennel leaves, to garnish

Place the fennel and 150 ml (¼ pint) water in a pan, cover and cook for 10 minutes.

Meanwhile, cut the fins and gills from the fish. To remove the bones turn the fish over, cut through the backbone at the head and tail, then carefully lift the backbone out. Remove any extra bones.

For the stuffing, soak the breadcrumbs in the milk then squeeze dry. Melt 30 g (1 oz) of the margarine in a pan and fry the shallots until soft. Stir into the breadcrumbs with the parsley, lemon rind, egg yolks and seasoning. Spoon the stuffing into the cavity in the fish and sew up with fine string or cotton or secure with wooden cocktail sticks.

Place the fish in a shallow, greased ovenproof dish and pour over the wine and vermouth. Drain the fennel and add to the dish. Dot the remaining margarine over the fish and season. Cover with greased greaseproof paper. Cook in a preheated oven at 170°C (325°F) mark 5 for 30–40 minutes or until the flesh flakes easily.

Carefully transfer the fish to a warmed serving plate. Remove the fennel from the cooking liquid with a slotted spoon and place on the dish with the fish. Cover and keep hot.

Strain the cooking liquid into a saucepan and boil until reduced to a light, syrupy consistency. Stir in the cream and continue to boil until slightly thickened. Adjust the seasoning. Remove the thread, or cocktail sticks, from the fish and spoon the sauce over. Garnish with fennel leaves and serve at once.

Baked scampi and spinach in Pernod sauce

Spinach, chard or lettuce leaves wrapped round fish or shellfish help retain the natural juices and flavour of the seafood.

Serves 4

    about 24 large spinach leaves, central ribs removed
    350 g (12 oz) peeled scampi tails
    30 g (1 oz) polyunsaturated margarine
    60 ml (4 tbsp) dry white wine
    pinch of cayenne
    salt and freshly ground pepper
    1 shallot, skinned and finely chopped
    60 ml (4 tbsp) Pernod
    150 ml (¼ pint) fish stock
    120 ml (4 fl oz) double cream
    30 ml (2 tbsp) grated Parmesan cheese

Pour boiling water over the spinach leaves. Drain, then immediately drop them into iced water. Dry well. Wrap the scampi in the leaves. Grease a shallow ovenproof dish with half the margarine and arrange the wrapped scampi in a single layer. Pour over the wine and add the cayenne and seasoning. Cover and bake in a preheated oven at 190°C (375°F) mark 5 for 20 minutes. Drain the juices and reserve. Transfer the scampi to a flameproof serving dish and keep hot.

Melt the remaining margarine and fry the shallot until soft. Stir in the Pernod and bring to the boil. Add the fish stock and pan juices and boil rapidly until reduced by half. Add the cream and continue boiling until reduced and thickened slightly. Adjust the seasoning. Pour the sauce over the scampi and sprinkle with the Parmesan cheese. Cook under a preheated hot grill until golden brown.

Salmon trout steaks with watercress sauce

This recipe may also be made with fresh salmon.

Serves 4

    300 ml (½ pint) dry white wine
    600 ml (1 pint) water
    1 bouquet garni

salt and 6 peppercorns
1 small onion, skinned and sliced
1 small carrot, peeled and sliced
30 ml (2 tbsp) double cream
175 g (6 oz) polyunsaturated margarine
2 bunches of watercress
4 salmon trout or salmon steaks
10 ml (2 tsp) lemon juice
½ lemon, thinly sliced, to garnish

Bring the wine, water, bouquet garni, seasoning, onion and carrot to the boil in a large shallow pan. Simmer for 20 minutes or until the vegetables are tender.

Strain 75 ml (3 fl oz) of the court bouillon into a small saucepan and boil until reduced by two-thirds. Stir in the double cream and boil gently for 2 minutes. Gradually whisk in the margarine.

Reserving four small sprigs and some large leaves for garnish, plunge the watercress, including the stalks, into boiling water. Drain immediately, then refresh in cold water. Drain and squeeze as much water as possible from the watercress. Chop the watercress finely and add it to the sauce. Keep hot.

Strain the remaining court bouillon and return it to the pan. Add the fish steaks and cook gently in the court bouillon for 12–15 minutes or until the flesh flakes easily. Drain.

Stir the lemon juice into the sauce. Arrange the reserved watercress leaves around the edge of each plate, pour over the sauce and place the fish on the top. Garnish with watercress sprigs and lemon slices.

Lobster Newburg

A ready-cooked lobster from your fishmonger may be used. A small lobster 700 g–1 kg (1½–2 lb) will serve two people as a main course.

Serves 2

> 700 g–1 kg (1½–2 lb) lobster, cooked
> 30 g (1 oz) polyunsaturated margarine
> 300 ml (½ pint) sherry
> about 150 ml (¼ pint) single cream
> 300 ml (½ pint) béchamel sauce
> 2 egg yolks
> button mushrooms, to garnish

Cut the meat of the lobster into pieces, reserving the half shells for serving. Heat the margarine in a pan and sauté the lobster for 1 minute. Add the sherry and stir briskly over the heat for another minute. Reduce the heat and pour in enough cream to coat all the pieces. Fold in the béchamel sauce. Beat the egg yolks into 30 ml (2 tbsp) cream and stir into the lobster mixture to bind. Fill the half lobster shells with the mixture and garnish with button mushrooms.

Lobster Espagnole

Serves 4

> 30 ml (2 tbsp) olive oil
> 2 medium onions, skinned and chopped
> 1 clove garlic, skinned and finely chopped
> 4 large tomatoes, seeded and skinned
> 50 ml (2 fl oz) sherry
> 700 g (1½ lb) cooked lobster meat, chopped
> 150 ml (¼ pint) chicken or fish stock
> salt and freshly ground pepper
> chopped fresh parsley, to garnish

Heat the oil in a large pan and gently fry the onions until soft but not browned. Add the garlic, tomatoes and sherry and cook until the tomatoes are soft. Add the lobster meat, stock and seasoning and heat through. Garnish with parsley and serve with boiled rice, salad and hot crusty bread.

Stuffed plaice with lemon sauce

Serves 4

4 small whole plaice, cleaned
75 g (2½ oz) polyunsaturated margarine
125 g (4 oz) button mushrooms, finely chopped
125 g (4 oz) white breadcrumbs
90 ml (6 tbsp) chopped fresh parsley
45 ml (3 tbsp) crushed green peppercorns
finely grated rind and juice of 2 lemons
1.25 ml (¼ tsp) mustard powder
salt and freshly ground pepper
1 egg, beaten
150 ml (¼ pint) dry white wine
30 g (1 oz) plain flour
60 ml (4 tbsp) single cream
lemon slices and parsley sprigs, to garnish

With the white skin uppermost, cut down the backbone of each plaice. Carefully make a pocket on each side of the backbone by easing the white flesh from the bone.

For the stuffing, beat 15 g (½ oz) of the margarine until softened, then add the mushrooms, breadcrumbs, parsley, 30 ml (2 tbsp) of the peppercorns, the lemon rind, mustard and seasoning to taste. Mix well and moisten with the egg and a little of the lemon juice.

Spoon the stuffing carefully into the pockets in the fish, then place the fish in a single layer in a greased baking dish. Pour the wine around the fish and cover loosely with foil. Cook in a preheated oven at 190°C (375°F) mark 5 for 30 minutes. Remove the fish and place on a warmed serving dish, reserving the cooking juices. Cover and keep warm.

For the sauce, melt the remaining margarine in a saucepan, add the flour and cook gently, stirring, for 1–2 minutes. Remove from the heat and gradually blend in the reserved fish cooking juices, 150 ml (¼ pint) water and the remaining lemon juice. Bring to the boil, stirring constantly, then lower the heat and stir in the remaining peppercorns and the cream. Taste and adjust the seasoning, then pour into a warmed sauceboat. Garnish the fish and serve with the sauce.

Paupiettes of sole with salmon mousseline

Fillets of sole, filled with a delicate salmon mousse and poached in vermouth, make an elegant and delectable dish.

Serves 4

>   4 sole fillets, skinned and cut in half lengthways
>   30 g (1 oz) polyunsaturated margarine
>   salt and freshly ground pepper
>   90 ml (6 tbsp) dry white vermouth
>   250 ml (8 fl oz) single cream
>   7.5 ml (1½ tsp) chopped fresh dill
>   10 ml (2 tsp) lemon juice
>   dill sprigs, to garnish

For the mousseline

>   225 g (8 oz) salmon fillet, skinned, boned, shredded and
>   chilled
>   1 egg white, chilled
>   90 ml (6 tbsp) double cream, chilled
>   5 ml (1 tsp) chopped fresh dill
>   7.5 ml (1½ tsp) lemon juice
>   salt and freshly ground pepper

For the mousseline, purée the salmon in a food processor until smooth, then add the egg white and mix again. Gradually add the double cream, mixing after each addition. Add the dill, lemon juice and seasoning.

Divide the mousseline between the eight sole fillets. Roll up and secure each one with a wooden cocktail stick.

Grease an ovenproof dish with the margarine and arrange the sole in a single layer. Season well, then pour in the vermouth and 60 ml (4 tbsp) water. Cover with foil and bake in a preheated oven at 190°C (375°F) mark 5 for 20 minutes until the fish is white and the mousseline firm. Transfer to a serving plate and keep hot.

Strain the juices into a saucepan and boil rapidly until reduced by half. Stir in the cream, chopped dill, lemon juice and seasoning. Simmer gently to reduce slightly. Do not boil. Remove the cocktail sticks from the sole, garnish with dill sprigs and serve with the sauce.

Salmon for a special occasion

Salmon is not only the acknowledged 'king' of fish, but it looks attractive, is easily boned and has a delightful flavour. As a result of farming, it is quite economical these days too. A 125 g (4 oz) portion has under 200 calories when steamed or poached. It can be cooked quickly and safely too, using several different techniques which retain the Omega-3 fatty acids and flavour. In addition to being a very rich source of the Omega-3 fatty acids which protect against heart attacks, salmon contains protein, calcium and iron as well as vitamins A and D, thiamin and riboflavin. It is a fish that children, who can be difficult with fish, will readily take a liking to. For the busy cook or housewife, it lends itself to dishes which can be prepared in advance and then quickly served on those occasions when time is limited.

The Laird's salmon with kumquats

Ideal for Christmas or a special occasion.

Serves 4

    1 kg (2 lb) Scottish salmon fillet, skinned
    15 g (½ oz) polyunsaturated margarine
    30 ml (2 tbsp) muscovado or soft brown sugar
    125 g (4 oz) kumquats, thinly sliced
    salt and freshly ground pepper
    200 ml (7 fl oz) dry cider
    15 ml (1 tbsp) Worcestershire sauce
    10 ml (2 tsp) cornflour

Cut the salmon fillet into four pieces and lay them in a large ovenproof dish. Dot with the margarine and sprinkle with the sugar. Scatter the kumquats over the salmon and season well. Reserve 30 ml (2 tbsp) cider and pour the remainder over the salmon with the Worcestershire sauce. Cover closely with a lid or foil. Bake in a preheated oven at 220°C (425°F) mark 7 for about 20 minutes.

Carefully pour off the liquid, with the kumquat slices, into a saucepan. Blend the cornflour with the reserved cider and stir into the pan. Stir over the heat until thickened slightly, then simmer for 2 minutes. Pour over the salmon and serve with fresh vegetables.

Scottish salmon stuffed with ginger

For a delightful meal with a hint of the exotic, the lemony stuffing is flavoured with ginger.

Serves 6–8

    1.6 kg (3½ lb) Scottish salmon, cut into 2 fillets, skinned
    finely grated rind and juice of 1 lemon
    5 cm (2 inch) piece of fresh root ginger, peeled and finely
        chopped
    90 g (3 oz) fresh brown breadcrumbs
    90 g (3 oz) ground almonds
    75 ml (5 tbsp) chopped fresh parsley
    1 egg, size 3, beaten
    salt and freshly ground pepper
    15 ml (1 tbsp) olive oil
    flaked almonds, to garnish

Place one piece of the salmon fillet on a large piece of non-stick paper or greased foil. Mix together the lemon rind and juice, ginger, breadcrumbs, ground almonds, parsley and egg. Season to taste. Press about a third of the mixture on to the salmon fillet, keeping to the centre, then place the second salmon fillet over to enclose. Brush with the oil to moisten. Shape the remaining stuffing into small balls.

Fold the paper or foil over the fish and tuck over ends to seal firmly. Place on a baking sheet. Bake in a preheated oven at 190°C (375°F) mark 5 for about 25 minutes, arranging the stuffing balls on the baking sheet halfway through the cooking time. Scatter the flaked almonds over and serve the salmon hot, in thick slices, with the stuffing balls and bean sprouts.

Scottish salmon filo parcels with pepper sauces

An easy dish to prepare in advance if you are entertaining. The parcels can be prepared earlier and refrigerated ready for baking and the sauces will keep in the refrigerator for up to two days. The paper-thin filo pastry is best worked quickly without giving it time to dry out.

Serves 6

> 9 standard sheets filo (phyllo) pastry
> olive oil or polyunsaturated margarine, melted, for brushing
> 6 x 150 g (5 oz) Scottish salmon steaks
> finely grated rind of 1 lemon
> 60 g (2 oz) polyunsaturated margarine
> freshly ground pepper
> coriander sprigs, to garnish

For the sauces

> 2 red peppers, seeded and chopped
> 2 yellow peppers, seeded and chopped
> 300 ml (½ pint) fish stock or water
> salt and freshly ground pepper

For the sauces, place the red and yellow peppers in separate pans with half the stock in each. Cover tightly and simmer gently until the peppers are soft. Purée the two batches separately in a blender or food processor, then press through a sieve. Season each sauce to taste.

Open out the sheets of filo pastry and cut each in half across the width. Brush each with oil or margarine and layer in stacks of three, making six squares of pastry. Place a piece of salmon on each piece of pastry. Mix the lemon rind with the margarine and black pepper, then divide this between the six salmon pieces. Fold the pastry over, enclosing the salmon like an envelope. Brush the parcels with oil or margarine and place on a baking sheet in a preheated oven at 225°C (425°F) mark 7 for about 12 minutes until golden and crisp.

Serve each parcel hot with a spoonful of each sauce on the plate, and a crisp green salad. Garnish with a sprig of coriander.

Scottish salmon cutlets with Highland whisky sauce

A delightful party dish to set the mood for the evening. The creamy whisky sauce is best finished at the last minute, but you can prepare it in advance as far as adding the fromage frais.

Serves 6

> 6 Scottish salmon cutlets
> 15 ml (1 tbsp) olive oil
> freshly ground pepper

For the sauce

> 45 ml (3 tbsp) olive oil
> 175 g (6 oz) button mushrooms, thinly sliced
> 175 ml (6 fl oz) whisky
> 175 g (6 oz) fromage frais

Place the salmon cutlets on a foil-lined grill pan, brush lightly with oil and sprinkle with pepper. Cook under a preheated moderate heat, turning once, for 8–10 minutes.

For the sauce, heat the oil in a pan and gently cook the mushrooms, stirring, for 3 minutes. Stir in the whisky and cook over a high heat until the liquid is reduced by about one-third. Reduce the heat and stir in the fromage frais, then heat gently. Serve the sauce with the grilled salmon cutlets and accompany with fresh vegetables.

New Year salmon en croûte

A sumptuous meal, yet not as expensive as it looks. Best with asparagus, but other green vegetables such as courgettes or broccoli are equally tasteful alternatives. Prepare ahead of the day and make life easier for yourself on New Year's Day – simple store in the refrigerator ready to bake.

Serves 6–8

225 g (8 oz) asparagus spears or small courgettes
salt and freshly ground pepper
30 g (1 oz) polyunsaturated margarine
finely grated rind of 1 medium orange
1.4 g (3 lb) Scottish salmon, filleted and skinned
450 g (1 lb) ready-made puff pastry
1 egg, beaten

For the sauce

30 g (1 oz) polyunsaturated margarine
30 g (1 oz) shallot or onion, skinned and finely chopped
120 ml (4 fl oz) dry white wine
juice of 1 medium orange
75 ml (5 tbsp) fromage frais
shredded orange rind, to garnish

Cook the asparagus spears or courgettes in a saucepan of lightly salted boiling water for 10–15 minutes or until tender. Drain well, then trim off the very tips of the asparagus or a few thin slices of courgette and set aside.

Mix the margarine with the orange rind and plenty of black pepper. Lay the salmon fillets out on a board and spread with the orange margarine. Arrange the asparagus spears, or courgettes, down the centre of one piece of salmon, then place the other on top, margarine side down.

Divide the pastry in half and roll out each to a rectangle about 20 x 30 cm (8 x 12 inches). Place the fish on one, brush the edges with egg and cover with the remaining pastry. Trim off excess pastry and pinch the edges together to seal. Use the trimmings to decorate. Place on a baking sheet and chill for 30 minutes.

Glaze the pastry with beaten egg. Bake in a preheated oven at 200°C (400°F) mark 6 for about 45 minutes until golden brown.

For the sauce, melt the margarine in a pan and fry the shallot until soft but not browned. Add the wine and simmer, uncovered, for 5 minutes. Stir in the orange juice and fromage frais and heat gently. Adjust the seasoning.

Serve the salmon warm or cold, in slices, garnished with the reserved asparagus tips and orange rind. Serve with sweetcorn and accompany with the orange sauce.

Wee Scottish salmon en papillote

Larger than trout but far smaller than the size traditionally associated with fully mature salmon, wee Scottish salmon weighs about 1–1½ kg (2½–3 lb). This makes an ideal size for family meals. Its versatility and easy preparation makes it a very attractive choice for the busy modern cook, yet is capable of producing gourmet meals.

Serves 4–5

> 225 g (8 oz) Greek strained yogurt
> juice of ½ medium lemon
> 30 ml (2 tbsp) clear honey
> 15 ml (1 tbsp) Meaux or similar coarse-grained mustard
> 1 clove garlic, skinned and crushed
> 30 ml (2 tbsp) chopped fresh dill
> 30 ml (2 tbsp) grated Parmesan cheese
> 2 wee Scottish salmon fillets, skinned
> 45 ml (3 tbsp) pine nuts, lightly toasted under the grill

Mix the yogurt, lemon juice, honey, mustard, garlic, dill and Parmesan together.

Lay two sheets of foil, each about 5 cm (2 inches) longer than the salmon fillets at each end. Put one of the fillets on a foil sheet and spread a third of the sauce over the fillet. Top with the other fillet, spread over another third of the sauce and sprinkle the toasted nuts over this. Cover with the second sheet of foil, roll up the edges all round to make a neat parcel and place on a baking sheet.

Bake in a preheated oven at 220°C (425°F) mark 7 for 20 minutes. Transfer the parcel to a serving dish. Slice open the parcel at the table for everyone to enjoy the fragrance, and serve each helping with a spoonful of the remaining sauce, new potatoes and a mixed salad. Enjoy any leftovers cold or at room temperature. Do not reheat.

Scottish salmon cutlets with avocado and brandy mayonnaise

The sauce can be made a day or two in advance and stored, covered closely, in the refrigerator.

Serves 4

1 small onion, skinned and sliced
1 small carrot, peeled and sliced
1 bay leaf
300 ml (½ pint) dry white wine
salt and freshly ground pepper
4 x 225 g (8 oz) Scottish salmon cutlets
parsley sprigs and shaped croûtons of bread, to garnish

For the sauce

1 large ripe avocado, peeled and stoned
150 ml (¼ pint) mayonnaise
15 ml (1 tbsp) lemon juice
45 ml (3 tbsp) brandy, whisky or dry sherry

Place the onion and carrot in a wide pan with the bay leaf, wine and seasoning. Bring to the boil, cover and simmer for 10 minutes. Add the salmon cutlets, cover and simmer over a very low heat for 7–8 minutes.

For the sauce, mash or purée the avocado in a food processor with the mayonnaise and lemon juice. Beat in the brandy.

Remove the salmon cutlets from the liquor and arrange on a warmed serving plate. Boil the liquor to reduce to about 30 ml (2 tbsp) and beat into the sauce. Adjust seasoning to taste and serve with the salmon. Garnish with sprigs of parsley and croûtons of bread, cut in holly leaf shapes and, if liked, serve with peas.

Non-fish Recipes

We would like these recipes to show you how much you *can* eat just as they will show you how to avoid the excess of saturated fat which is unhealthy. We recommend that you eat animal meat as a main meal no more than twice a week. If necessary, refresh your memory of the advice on meat and the general tips on cutting down fat in cooking given in chapter 4. We have included some sample meat dishes in this section to show you how to do this, but on the whole we devote our attentions to alternative dishes, such as those made from poultry and vegetables.

Reducing the saturated fat in the Sunday joint

Red meat will always contain cholesterol in the meat itself no matter how lean it is. This is why we suggest you eat this no more than twice a week as a main meal. Pick a lean joint of meat but remember that some fat is necessary in order to cook the meat successfully. Use as little oil as possible when cooking and avoid adding hard fat such as lard, dripping, butter or ghee. A very lean joint can be baked in foil to keep it moist during cooking.

A good deal of the fat comes out of the meat during normal roasting. This can be removed from the meat juices before preparing the gravy. Strain the juices into a sauce-pan or heatproof jug and add very cold water. The fat will tend to solidify on top and can then be removed. It may be necessary to put the mixture in the fridge for a while, but make sure the liquid has reached room temperature before doing so. You should never put hot food in the fridge as this will raise the temperature and result in spoiling. Adding iced water to the meat juices after cooking will achieve the same result.

To prepare the gravy, use the fat-reduced meat juices and add as much water as necessary. Heat a little and thicken with Bisto or cornflour, or a combination of the two. Do not make gravy with beef dripping or other hard fats.

Avoid roasting potatoes in the full-fat meat juices. Potatoes can be roasted in vegetable oil but baking or boiling them is an even better option.

Chicken Véronique

Using skinned chicken and low-fat yogurt helps reduce the fat content of this dish.

Serves 4

    15 ml (1 tbsp) olive oil
    4 x 125–175 g (4–6 oz) chicken pieces, skinned
    1 medium onion, skinned and sliced
    125 g (4 oz) button mushrooms
    pared rind and juice of 1 lemon
    150 ml (¼ pint) chicken stock
    150 ml (¼ pint) dry white wine
    salt and freshly ground pepper
    175 g (6 oz) seedless grapes
    15 ml (1 tbsp) cornflour
    30 ml (2 tbsp) low-fat natural yogurt

Heat the oil in a non-stick frying pan and cook the chicken for about 2 minutes or until lightly browned on both sides. Put into a large casserole. Add the onion and mushrooms to the pan and cook for 3 minutes until the onion is soft. Add the lemon rind and juice, stock, wine and seasoning. Bring to the boil and simmer for 2 minutes, then pour over the chicken.

Cover and cook in a preheated oven at 190°C (375°F) mark 5 for 40 minutes until the juices run clear when the thickest part of the chicken is pierced. Add 125 g (4 oz) of the grapes and continue cooking for 5 minutes. Using a slotted spoon, transfer the chicken, onion, mushrooms and grapes to a serving dish and keep hot.

Strain off 300 ml (½ pint) of the cooking liquid and put in a pan, skimming off any fat. Blend the cornflour with a little water, then stir in a little of the hot cooking liquid. Add to the pan and cook for about 2 minutes, stirring, until thickened. Remove from the heat and stir in the yogurt. Pour over the chicken and garnish with the remaining grapes. Serve with new potatoes and French beans.

Chicken salad

Serves 4–6

    700 g (1½ lb) cooked chicken, skinned, boned and shredded
    425 g (15 oz) can red kidney beans, drained and rinsed
    2 oranges, peeled and segmented, with rind cut into strips
    125 g (4 oz) button mushrooms, sliced
    3 spring onions, trimmed and finely chopped
    60 g (2 oz) walnut halves
    salt and freshly ground pepper
    225 g (8 oz) spinach leaves, washed and shredded
    ½ crisp lettuce, shredded
    ½ green pepper, seeded and sliced

For the dressing

    ½ cucumber, grated and drained
    150 ml (¼ pint) low-fat natural yogurt
    15 ml (1 tbsp) lemon juice
    little paprika

Mix the chicken and beans in a bowl. Add the orange segments, rind, mushrooms, onions, walnuts and seasoning.

Mix the spinach, lettuce and green pepper in a large serving bowl and place the chicken mixture on top.

Combine the dressing ingredients and serve in a separate bowl.

Baked gingered chicken

Serves 4

> 4 small chicken portions, skinned
> 10 ml (2 tsp) soy sauce
> 30 ml (2 tbsp) dry sherry
> 60 ml (4 tbsp) unsweetened apple juice
> 2 lemon slices, finely chopped
> 1 clove garlic, skinned and crushed
> 10 ml (2 tsp) grated fresh root ginger

Arrange the chicken in a baking dish just large enough to take the pieces in one layer, fleshy side down. Mix the rest of the ingredients together and pour over the chicken. Cover and leave to marinate for several hours.

Bake in a preheated oven at 200°C (400°F) mark 6 for 30–40 minutes or until the juices run clear when a skewer is inserted into the thickest part. Turn the chicken halfway through cooking and baste frequently.

Fruity turkey braise

Serves 4

> 2 large turkey legs, about 700–800 kg (1½–1¾ lb) total weight, skinned
> 10 ml (2 tsp) wholemeal flour
> 15 ml (1 tbsp) olive oil
> 1 medium onion, skinned and chopped
> 10 ml (2 tsp) finely chopped fresh root ginger
> 450 ml (¾ pint) chicken stock
> 2.5 ml (½ tsp) ground allspice
> 2.5 ml (½ tsp) ground cinnamon
> 1 cooking apple, peeled, cored and chopped
> 1 firm ripe pear, peeled, cored and chopped
> 1 red pepper, seeded and chopped
> salt and freshly ground pepper

Dust the turkey legs with the flour. Heat the oil in a flameproof casserole and cook the turkey on all sides for about 8–10 minutes until lightly browned. Remove from the casserole and set aside.

Add the onion and ginger to the casserole and fry for 5 minutes until soft. Stir in the stock, allspice and cinnamon and bring to the boil. Return the turkey legs to the casserole, cover tightly and cook gently for 45 minutes.

Add the apple, pear, red pepper and seasoning. Cook for a further 45 minutes or until the turkey is tender. Remove the turkey legs from the casserole and slice the meat from the bone. Skim off any fat from the surface of the sauce, then return the pieces of meat to warm through. Serve hot.

Turkey fillets with mushrooms

Turkey fillets filled with delicious herby mushrooms, rolled and then braised.
Serves 4

    4 turkey fillets, about 150 g (5 oz) each
    15 ml (1 tbsp) olive oil
    1 medium onion, skinned and finely chopped
    175 g (6 oz) mushrooms, chopped
    1 clove garlic, skinned and crushed
    5 ml (1 tsp) finely grated lemon rind
    10 ml (2 tsp) chopped fresh thyme or 5 ml (1 tsp) dried thyme
    15 ml (1 tbsp) capers, well drained and chopped
    salt and freshly ground pepper
    300 ml (½ pint) hot chicken stock
    30 ml (2 tbsp) lemon juice
    15 ml (1 tbsp) chopped fresh parsley
    lemon slices and parsley sprigs, to garnish

Cut each turkey fillet in half crossways and place each half between sheets of greaseproof paper. Beat until the fillets measure about 10 x 15 cm (4 x 6 inches).

Heat 5 ml (1 tsp) of the oil in a non-stick frying pan and cook the onion and mushrooms for 5–10 minutes over a gentle heat until excess moisture has evaporated. Remove from the heat and add the garlic, lemon rind, thyme and capers. Season to taste and mix well.

Divide the mushroom mixture into eight and spread over the fillets. Roll up and secure at both ends with string.

Heat the remaining oil in a non-stick frying pan just large

enough to hold the eight rolls. Cook the rolls, four at a time, for about 5 minutes each batch, turning until pale golden on all sides. Return all the rolls to the pan with the stock and lemon juice. Cover and simmer gently for 20 minutes.

Transfer the rolls to a serving plate, remove the string and keep warm. Boil the pan juices until reduced, then stir in the parsley and pour over the turkey rolls. Serve garnished with lemon slices and parsley sprigs.

Turkey meatballs in egg and lemon sauce

Serves 4

2 thick slices of wholemeal bread, crusts removed
45 ml (3 tbsp) dry white wine
salt and freshly ground pepper
15 ml (1 tbsp) chopped fresh tarragon
1 egg
225 g (8 oz) skinless, boneless turkey, minced
750 ml (1¼ pints) chicken stock

For the sauce

15 g (½ oz) cornflour
juice of 1 lemon
1 egg

For the meatballs, put the bread, 45 ml (3 tbsp) water and the wine in a bowl and beat well with a fork until smooth. Beat in the black pepper, tarragon, egg and turkey. Chill the mixture in the refrigerator for several hours until firm.

Divide the mixture into 20 pieces and form into neat, firm meatballs with wet hands.

Bring the stock to the boil in a saucepan. Add the meatballs in two batches, simmering gently, covered, for 7 minutes. Remove the meatballs to a warmed serving dish. Keep warm, reserving the stock.

For the sauce, mix together the cornflour and lemon juice. Beat in the egg and add the reserved stock. Heat gently, whisking rapidly all the time. Simmer for 1–2 minutes, then strain the sauce over the meatballs.

Chicken with mustard sauce

Serves 4

    4 x 175 g (6 oz) chicken portions, skinned
    20 ml (4 tsp) whole grain mustard
    juice of 1 small lemon
    150 ml (¼ pint) low-fat natural yogurt
    fresh coriander leaves or chopped fresh parsley, to garnish

Put the chicken in a roasting tin and spread the mustard equally on each portion. Sprinkle over the lemon juice. Roast in a preheated oven at 200°C (400°F) mark 6 for about 40 minutes, turning once, until cooked.

Remove the chicken with a slotted spoon, arrange on warmed serving plates and keep warm. Add the yogurt to the roasting tin and stir to mix with any juices and excess mustard from the base of the tin. Heat the sauce without boiling, stirring, then pour over the chicken. Garnish with fresh coriander or chopped parsley.

Piquant chicken

Serves 4

    15 ml (1 tbsp) olive oil
    4 chicken breasts, each weighing 125 g (4 oz), skinned
    1 large onion, skinned and finely chopped
    10 ml (2 tsp) ground ginger
    15 ml (1 tbsp) Dijon mustard
    30 g (1 oz) wholemeal flour
    450 ml (¾ pint) vegetable or chicken stock
    60 ml (4 tbsp) dry sherry
    175 g (6 oz) button mushrooms, roughly chopped
    salt and freshly ground pepper
    watercress sprigs, to garnish

Heat the oil in a large non-stick saucepan and cook the chicken breasts until evenly browned. Remove with a slotted spoon, place in a large casserole and keep warm.

Add the onion to the pan and cook for 5 minutes until

soft. Add the ginger and mustard, stir well, then add the flour. Cook for a few minutes, then remove from the heat and stir in the stock and sherry. Return to the heat and bring to the boil, stirring. Add the mushrooms, and season to taste. Pour the sauce over the chicken breasts. Cook in a preheated oven at 180°C (350°F) mark 4 for 50 minutes or until tender.

Place the chicken breasts in a serving dish and keep warm. Quickly reduce the sauce a little by boiling. Pour over the chicken and garnish with watercress.

Middle-Eastern stuffed chicken

Dried fruits are an excellent source of fibre and minerals. Serve the chicken with saffron rice.

Serves 4

   15 ml (1 tbsp) olive oil
   1 small onion, skinned and finely chopped
   60 g (2 oz) raisins
   60 g (2 oz) no-soak dried stoned prunes, chopped
   30 g (1 oz) blanched almonds, chopped
   1 eating apple, peeled, cored and finely chopped
   2.5 ml (½ tsp) ground allspice
   2.5 ml (½ tsp) ground cinnamon
   30 ml (2 tbsp) lemon juice
   salt and freshly ground pepper
   1.4 kg (3 lb) chicken

Heat the oil in a small non-stick saucepan and cook the onion for about 5 minutes until lightly browned.

Mix together the raisins, prunes, almonds, apple and spices in a bowl. Add the onion and 15 ml (1 tbsp) of the lemon juice. Season to taste and mix well. Stuff the neck of the chicken with the fruit mixture. Place the chicken in a roasting tin, season and sprinkle with the remaining lemon juice.

Roast in a preheated oven at 190°C (375°F) mark 5 for 1¼ hours or until browned and the juices run clear when a skewer is inserted into the thickest part of the leg.

Chicken in a pot

The liquid left in the pot can be skimmed and used to make chicken soup, or used as chicken stock for another dish. It will keep in the refrigerator for 2–3 days, or in the freezer for several months.

Serves 4

    1.4 kg (3 lb) chicken, skinned
    225 g (8 oz) celeriac, peeled, trimmed and cut into large chunks
    225 g (8 oz) carrots, peeled and cut into large chunks
    3 sticks of celery, cut into large chunks
    1 small onion, skinned and sliced
    30 ml (2 tbsp) chopped fresh thyme or 15 ml (1 tbsp)
      dried thyme
    2 cloves garlic, skinned and crushed
    15 ml (1 tbsp) lemon juice
    salt and freshly ground pepper
    chopped fresh parsley, to garnish

Put all the ingredients, except the parsley, in a large flameproof pot and add 600 ml (1 pint) water. Cover and simmer for 1 hour or until the chicken is cooked and the juices run clear when a skewer is inserted into the thickest part of the leg.

Remove the chicken and vegetables with a slotted spoon and arrange on a warmed platter. Garnish with parsley.

Chicken in yogurt and spices

Serves 4

    300 ml (½ pint) low-fat natural yogurt
    15 ml (1 tbsp) freshly ground coriander
    15 ml (1 tbsp) freshly ground cumin
    1 cm (½ inch) piece of fresh root ginger, peeled and finely
      chopped, or 10 ml (2 tsp) ground ginger
    5 ml (1 tsp) chilli powder
    1 clove garlic, skinned and crushed
    4 x 300 g (10 oz) chicken breasts on the bone, skinned
    coriander sprigs, to garnish

Mix the yogurt, coriander, cumin, ginger, chilli and garlic together in a bowl. Prick the chicken breasts all over with a fork and spread with half of the yogurt mixture. Cover and marinate for at least 3–4 hours or overnight in the refrigerator, turning occasionally.

Transfer the chicken to a roasting tin. Bake in a preheated oven at 200°C (400°F) mark 6 for 45 minutes. Remove from the tin and keep warm. Put the roasting tin over a gentle heat, stir in the reserved yogurt mixture and heat through, but do not boil, scraping up any sediment and juices from the base of the pan. Pour the sauce over the chicken and serve hot, garnished with coriander sprigs.

Jerusalem chicken

Serves 4

Jerusalem artichokes give this chicken dish a nutty flavour. Use them as soon as possible after buying as they quickly lose their lovely creamy colour.

   15 ml (1 tbsp) wholemeal flour
   salt and freshly ground pepper
   4 x 175–225 g (6–8 oz) chicken breasts, skinned
   15 ml (1 tbsp) olive oil
   2 medium onions, skinned and chopped
   300 ml (½ pint) chicken or vegetable stock, plus 15–30 ml
      (1–2 tbsp) extra, if necessary
   grated rind and juice of 1 lemon
   4 thyme sprigs or 2.5 ml (½ tsp) dried thyme
   450 g (1 lb) Jerusalem artichokes
   1 small red pepper, seeded and thinly sliced
   chopped fresh parsley, to garnish

Mix the flour with the seasoning and use to lightly coat the chicken breasts. Heat the oil in a large non-stick frying pan and cook the chicken breasts for 3 minutes on each side or until golden brown. Remove and drain well on absorbent kitchen paper. Pour the hot oil into a large non-stick saucepan and gently cook the onions for 3–5 minutes until soft but not browned. Pour in the stock with the lemon rind and juice and thyme.

Peel the artichokes and cut into slices or dice. Place in the pan at once and add the red pepper. Bring to the boil, then add the chicken. Cover and simmer gently for 30–40 minutes or until the chicken is tender and the artichokes are soft.

Remove the chicken to a warmed serving dish and keep hot. Reserve some of the pepper slices for garnish and discard the thyme sprigs. Purée the remaining vegetables and stock in a blender or food processor until smooth.

Reheat the sauce and season to taste, adding a little stock to thin if necessary. Pour the sauce over the chicken. Garnish with the reserved pepper and chopped parsley.

Spanish chicken and rice

Serves 4

> 4 chicken portions, halved
> 30 ml (2 tbsp) plain flour
> salt and freshly ground pepper
> 45 ml (3 tbsp) olive oil
> 1 medium onion, skinned and chopped
> 400 g (14 oz) can tomatoes
> 175 g (6 oz) can pimentos, drained and sliced
> 2 chicken stock cubes, crumbled
> 8 stuffed olives
> 175 g (6 oz) long grain rice
> 125 g (4 oz) smoked ham, chopped
> 125 g (4 oz) frozen peas
> watercress sprigs, to garnish

Toss the chicken in the flour seasoned with salt and pepper. Heat the oil in a large saucepan and brown the chicken on all sides, then remove. Add the onion and fry until golden brown.

Drain the tomatoes and add enough water to make the juice up to 450 ml (¾ pint). Return the chicken to the pan. Add the tomato juice, the tomatoes, pimentos, stock cubes, olives, rice and ham. Season to taste. Cover the pan tightly and simmer gently for 45 minutes, stirring carefully through the rice occasionally to prevent sticking.

Add the peas to the pan, cover again and simmer for a further 30 minutes until the chicken is tender. Before serving, adjust seasoning and garnish with the watercress.

Chicken and cheese salad

Serves 4

60 g (2 oz) blanched almonds
450 g (1 lb) cooked chicken meat, skinned
225 g (8 oz) low-fat cottage cheese
30 ml (2 tbsp) finely chopped fresh parsley
freshly ground pepper, to taste
lettuce leaves, to serve

Put the almonds on a sheet of foil and cook under a preheated hot grill, stirring continuously, for 1–2 minutes or until lightly golden brown. Set aside to cool.

Meanwhile, finely dice or shred the chicken and put in a bowl with the cottage cheese, parsley and black pepper. Add the almonds and gently mix together. Serve on lettuce.

DESSERT RECIPES

Baked apples

Serves 4

4 medium cooking apples
125 g (4 oz) sultanas
45 ml (3 tbsp) water
60 ml (4 tbsp) low-fat ice cream, to serve (optional)

Core the cooking apples and prick the skins to stop them bursting. Stand the apples in a microwave-proof dish and fill with sultanas. Surround with water and microwave on HIGH for 2½ minutes. Remove from the oven, cover with foil and leave to stand for a few minutes. Serve with ice cream, if liked.

Raspberry surprise

Serves 4

> 225 g (8 oz) raspberries
> 150 ml (¼ pint) low-fat natural yogurt
> 20 ml (4 tsp) honey

Put four raspberries in the base of each of four sundae glasses. Add about 40 ml (8 tsp) yogurt and 5 ml (1 tsp) honey to each glass and top with raspberries.

Peach pavlova

Serves 5

> 3 egg whites
> 175 g (6 oz) caster sugar

For the peach custard

> 60 g (2 oz) caster sugar
> 30 g (1 oz) cornflour
> 15 g (½ oz) custard powder
> 250 ml (8 fl oz) skimmed milk
> 2 x 425 g (15 oz) cans unsweetened peaches, drained

Put a sheet of greaseproof paper on a baking sheet and draw an 18 cm (7 inch) circle on it. Beat the egg whites in a large bowl with an electric mixer until soft peaks form. Gradually add the sugar and beat until dissolved. Spread half the egg white mixture over the circle. Alternatively, put in a piping bag fitted with a large nozzle and pipe the egg white mixture in circles to cover the area marked. Thicken the edge with the remaining egg white. Bake in a preheated oven at 150°C (300°F) mark 2 for about 1½ hours or until dry to the touch. Turn the heat off and leave the pavlova in the oven with the door ajar.

Blend the sugar, cornflour and custard powder together with a little of the milk. Heat the remaining milk in a pan until almost boiling. Pour the milk on to the custard mixture and stir well. Pour the custard back into the pan and bring to the boil, stirring. Cook, stirring, for 2–3 mintues until thickened. Cool. Drain the peaches and place half on the pavlova. Pour the custard over and decorate with the remaining peaches. Serve cold.

Slimline orange sorbet

Serves 4

   1 large orange
   175 ml (6 fl oz) orange juice
   300 ml (½ pint) natural yogurt
   15 g (½ oz) powdered gelatine
   2 egg whites
   mint sprigs, to decorate

Finely grate the rind from the orange and add to the orange juice, then mix in the yogurt. Dissolve the gelatine in 60 ml (4 tbsp) hot water in a bowl over a pan of simmering water. Blend with the orange and yogurt mixture and leave to thicken. Whisk the egg whites until stiff. When the yogurt mixture has thickened, fold the whites in carefully.

Peel the pith of the orange and divide the flesh into segments. Spoon the sorbet mixture into individual glasses and add the orange segments. Chill. Serve decorated with a sprig of mint in each glass.

Grape poached pears

Serves 2

   2 medium firm pears
   60 ml (4 tbsp) red grape juice
   7.5 ml (1½ tsp) caster sugar
   grated rind of ¼ lemon

Peel the pears, cut in half, core and remove the stringy fibres. Place the pears in a saucepan, pour in the grape juice and add the sugar and lemon rind. Cover and poach gently over a low heat for 12–15 minutes. Serve hot or cold.

Pineapple dessert

Serves 2

> 225 g (8 oz) canned pineapple with 60 ml (4 tbsp) juice
> 150 ml (¼ pint) low-fat natural yogurt
> 5 ml (1 tsp) demerara sugar
> 2.5 ml (½ tsp) ground mixed spice

Place the pineapple in a food processor and blend with the juice. Divide into two flameproof dishes. Spoon over the yogurt. Mix the sugar and spice and sprinkle over the yogurt. Place under a preheated hot grill until the sugar has melted. Serve hot.

Flamed Jamaican bananas

Serves 4

> 4 large under-ripe bananas
> 45 g (1½ oz) polyunsaturated margarine
> juice of ½ large lemon
> 30 ml (2 tbsp) rum
> brown sugar, to serve

Peel the bananas and halve lengthways. Heat the margarine in a flameproof dish and fry the bananas, cut sides down. When golden, turn over, sprinkle with lemon juice and fry the second side until golden. Warm the rum in a small heatproof dish, ignite and pour over the bananas. Serve while still flaming with a little brown sugar.

Spiced pears

Serves 4

4 large firm pears
½ lemon
16 cloves
½ cinnamon stick
300 ml (½ pint) red wine
30 ml (2 tbsp) redcurrant jelly
4 orange slices

Peel the pears, leaving the stalks on, and rub them all over with the lemon to prevent discoloration. Stud each pear with four cloves and stand them upright in a pan. Add the cinnamon stick, wine and sufficient water to cover the pears. Bring to the boil and simmer gently until the pears are tender. Leave to cool in the cooking liquid.

Put 30 ml (2 tbsp) of the cooking liquid into a small pan with the redcurrant jelly and cook quickly for about 1 minute until the jelly has dissolved. Place an orange slice in the middle of each serving dish. Drain the pears with a slotted spoon and place a pear on top of each orange slice. Spoon over a little of the redcurrant jelly mixture to glaze.

Mixed fruit teabread

This is a delicious cake with all the richness and flavour of a fruit cake while containing virtually no saturated fat.

175 g (6 oz) raisins
125 g (4 oz) sultanas
60 g (2 oz) currants
125 g (4 oz) light brown soft sugar
300 ml (½ pint) cold tea
1 egg, beaten
45 ml (3 tbsp) golden syrup
225 g (8 oz) plain wholemeal flour
7.5 ml (1½ tsp) baking powder
2.5 ml (½ tsp) ground mixed spice

Soak the dried fruit and sugar in the tea overnight. Grease and base-line a 1.6 litre (2¾ pint) loaf tin.

Beat the egg and syrup into the fruit mixture. Add the flour, baking powder and spice, mixing well. Spoon into the prepared tin. Bake in a preheated oven at 170°C (325°F) mark 3 for 30 minutes. Cover loosely with foil and cook for 40–60 minutes until well risen and just firm. Turn on to a wire rack to cool. Wrap in foil. Eat after 1–2 days.

French apple and ginger cake

This cake should be baked the day before required and chilled overnight.

Makes a 20 cm (8 inch) cake

225 g (8 oz) caster sugar
150 ml (¼ pint) cider
30 ml (2 tbsp) ginger syrup
pieces of thin lemon rind
900 g (2 lb) dessert apples
60 g (2 oz) sultanas
60 g (2 oz) chopped preserved ginger

Line the base of a 20 cm (8 inch) cake tin with foil and brush all over with olive oil. Dissolve the sugar in the cider and 150 ml (¼ pint) water. Add the ginger syrup and lemon rind and bring to the boil. Wash and core the apples, slice thinly and add to the syrup. Simmer very gently, uncovered, until transparent. Stir occasionally, taking care not to break up the slices. When cooked, lift them out of the syrup and drain.

Arrange the apple slices in layers in the cake tin. Sprinkle each layer with sultanas and chopped ginger. When all the apple is used up, cover with a heavy oil plate which fits closely to the top of the tin. Chill overnight.

To serve, remove the plate, place a large platter over the tin and invert it quickly. Carefully remove the tin and foil.

Oaty bars

Makes 18

90 g (3 oz) polyunsaturated margarine
30 ml (2 tbsp) skimmed milk
15 ml (1 tbsp) clear honey
90 g (3 oz) wholemeal flour
2.5 ml (½ tsp) bicarbonate of soda
2.5 ml (½ tsp) sugar
90 g (3 oz) rolled oats

Melt the margarine with the milk and honey in a saucepan. Put the flour, bicarbonate of soda, sugar and oats in a bowl. Mix together, then make a well in the centre. Pour in the melted margarine mixture and combine well. Divide the mixture into 18 portions and mould each portion into a bar about 6.5 cm (2½ inches) long. Place on two non-stick paper-lined baking sheets.

Bake in a preheated oven at 170°C (325°F) mark 3 for 20 minutes or until golden. Leave to cool for 2–3 minutes, then transfer to wire racks to cool completely.

VEGETABLE AND SALAD RECIPES

The whole point of eating vegetable dishes as part of the Eskimo diet is to reduce our consumption of saturated fat while allowing us a good intake of fibre, vitamins and essential minerals. It is important to remember that vegetarian does not necessarily mean low fat – dairy products in particular, with full-fat milk, creams and cheeses, are very high in saturated fat. This should always be kept in mind when planning vegetable dishes.

Minestrone soup

Serves 8

60 ml (4 tbsp) olive oil
1 large onion, skinned and chopped
1–2 cloves garlic, skinned and crushed
3 sticks of celery, finely chopped
3 carrots, peeled and finely chopped
2 courgettes, finely chopped
450 g (1 lb) tomatoes, skinned, or 400 g (14 oz) can tomatoes
125 g (4 oz) French or runner beans
125 g (4 oz) green cabbage, shredded
1.7 litres (3 pints) vegetable stock
salt and freshly ground pepper
120 ml (8 tbsp) chopped fresh parsley
400 g (14 oz) can cannellini beans, drained
60 g (2 oz) wholewheat spaghetti, broken into 1 cm (½ inch)
   pieces
grated Parmesan cheese, to serve

Heat the oil in a large flameproof casserole or saucepan and cook the onion and garlic until soft and beginning to turn golden. Add the remaining vegetables and stir well to mix.

Add the stock, seasoning and parsley. Bring to the boil, cover and simmer very gently for about 45 minutes or until all the vegetables are nearly tender. Stir in the cannellini beans and spaghetti and simmer for 15 minutes. Season. Serve sprinkled with grated Parmesan.

Thick bean and vegetable soup

Serves 6–8

225 g (8 oz) haricot beans, soaked overnight
45 ml (3 tbsp) olive oil
1 onion, skinned and chopped
1 clove of garlic, skinned and crushed
1 stick of celery, chopped

2 leeks, trimmed, washed and thinly sliced
450 g (1 lb) green cabbage, finely shredded
rosemary sprig and thyme sprig
15 ml (1 tbsp) tomato purée
salt and freshly ground pepper
30 ml (2 tbsp) chopped fresh parsley

Drain the beans and place in a large saucepan. Add 1.8 litres (3 pints) cold water, bring to the boil, cover and simmer for about 2 hours or until tender.

Heat the oil in a large saucepan and gently fry the onion, garlic and celery for 10 minutes, stirring frequently. Add the leeks, cabbage and herbs. Cook over a low heat, stirring all the time, for 4 minutes.

Drain the beans and add the cooking liquid to the vegetables together with the tomato purée. Season to taste. Bring to the boil and simmer for about 30 minutes. Add the beans, with more water if necessary, and simmer until the vegetables are tender. Remove the herbs and adjust seasoning. Stir in the parsley and serve immediately with hot crusty bread.

Spicy chick-peas and swede

Serves 4

225 g (8 oz) dried chick-peas, soaked overnight
225 g (8 oz) swede, peeled and roughly chopped
salt and freshly ground pepper
15–30 ml (1–2 tbsp) olive oil
1 medium onion, skinned and roughly chopped
5 ml (1 tsp) cumin seeds
2.5 ml (½ tsp) dried oregano
10 ml (2 tsp) paprika
15 ml (1 tbsp) plain flour
450 g (1 lb) tomatoes, roughly chopped
60 g (2 oz) medium-fat cheese, grated

Drain the chick-peas and rinse under running cold water. Put in a large saucepan, cover with plenty of fresh cold water and slowly bring to the boil. Cover and simmer for 45 minutes or until just tender. Drain well.

Put the swede into a saucepan and cover with cold salted water. Bring to the boil and simmer for 15–20 minutes or until tender. Drain, reserving 150 ml (¼ pint) of the cooking liquid.

Heat the oil in a medium saucepan and fry the onion, cumin, oregano and paprika for 1–2 minutes. Stir in the flour. Cook, stirring, for 1–2 minutes, then gradually stir in the reserved liquid. Bring to the boil, then stir in the tomatoes. Cover and simmer for 2–3 minutes. Add the chick-peas and swede and stir over a gentle heat for a few minutes until hot. Season to taste and top with a sprinkling of cheese.

Red kidney bean hot-pot

Serves 2

> 30 g (1 oz) polyunsaturated margarine
> 1 medium onion, skinned and roughly chopped
> 125 g (4 oz) celery, sliced
> 125 g (4 oz) carrots, peeled and sliced
> 15 ml (1 tbsp) plain flour
> 300 ml (½ pint) vegetable stock
> salt and freshly ground pepper
> 125 g (4 oz) runner beans, trimmed
> 125 g (4 oz) courgettes, sliced
> 400 g (14 oz) can red kidney beans, drained
> 30 g (1 oz) fresh wholemeal breadcrumbs
> 90 g (3 oz) Cheddar cheese, grated

Melt the margarine in a large saucepan and gently fry the onion for about 5 minutes until soft. Add the celery and carrots, cover and gently cook for 5 minutes. Add the flour and gently cook, stirring, for 1–2 minutes. Remove from the heat and gradually blend in the stock. Bring to the boil, stirring constantly, then simmer for 5 minutes. Season to taste. Add the runner beans and simmer for a further 5 minutes, then add the courgettes. Cook for a further 5–10 minutes until the vegetables are tender but still with a bite to them.

Add the kidney beans to the vegetables and heat through for about 5 minutes. Taste and adjust the seasoning. Turn the vegetable and bean mixture into a deep flameproof dish.

Mix the breadcrumbs and cheese together. Sprinkle on top of the bean mixture. Brown under a preheated hot grill until crisp and crusty. Serve hot, accompanied with whole-meal bread and a green salad.

Vegetable curry

Serves 4

    30 ml (2 tbsp) olive oil
    10 ml (2 tsp) ground coriander
    5 ml (1 tsp) ground cumin
    2.5–5 ml (½–1 tsp) chilli powder
    2.5 ml (½ tsp) ground turmeric
    2 cloves garlic, skinned and crushed
    1 medium onion, skinned and chopped
    1 small cauliflower, cut into small florets
    2 potatoes, peeled and roughly chopped
    2 carrots, peeled and sliced
    1 green pepper, seeded and chopped
    225 g (8 oz) tomatoes, roughly chopped
    150 ml (¼ pint) low-fat natural yogurt
    salt and freshly ground pepper

Heat the oil in a large saucepan and fry the coriander, cumin, chilli, tumeric, garlic and onion for 2–3 minutes, stirring continuously. Add the cauliflower, potatoes, carrots and green pepper and stir to coat in the spices. Stir in the tomatoes and 150 ml (¼ pint) water. Bring to the boil, cover and gently simmer for 25–30 minutes or until the vegetables are tender.

Remove from the heat, stir in the yogurt and season to taste. Serve with rice and chutney.

Broccoli and pasta salad

Serves 4

175 g (6 oz) wholewheat pasta spirals
300 g (10 oz) broccoli florets and chopped stems
15 ml (1 tbsp) sesame seeds
20 ml (4 tsp) olive oil
1 orange, peeled, segmented and chopped, with any juice
    reserved
salt and freshly ground pepper

Put the pasta in a saucepan half filled with boiling water.
Bring back to the boil and place the broccoli in a sieve over
the pan. Cover and cook for about 8 minutes or until the
pasta and broccoli are tender. Drain and place in a large
bowl.

Place the sesame seeds in an ungreased heavy-based
frying pan and cook over a low heat for 2–3 minutes or until
the seeds are just beginning to jump. Remove the seeds and
crush them in a pestle and mortar or grind them in a coffee
grinder.

Mix together the sesame seeds, oil, orange pieces and
any remaining orange juice in serving bowl. Add the
broccoli and pasta, then season to taste and toss gently.
Cover and chill before serving.

Wholewheat pasta with ratatouille sauce

An alternative ratatouille dish with a very low fat (and
calorie) content. Served with wholemeal pasta, this makes a
very satisfying and nourishing meal.

Serves 4–6

1–2 cloves garlic, skinned and crushed
1 large onion, preferably Spanish, skinned and chopped
450 g (1 lb) courgettes, sliced
1 large aubergine, sliced
1 medium green pepper, seeded and chopped

1 medium red pepper, seeded and chopped
450 g (1 lb) tomatoes, skinned and chopped or 400 g (14 oz)
    can chopped tomatoes
15 ml (1 tbsp) chopped fresh oregano or basil
salt and freshly ground pepper
wholewheat pasta, to serve

Put all the ingredients, except the pasta, into a large saucepan. Stir gently and cook over a low heat for 30–40 minutes until the vegetables are cooked. Taste and season.

Meanwhile, cook the pasta in a saucepan of boiling salted water according to the instructions on the packet. Drain and place in a warmed serving dish. Pour the sauce on top and serve immediately.

Vegetarian medley

Serves 4

15 ml (1 tbsp) olive oil
2 carrots, peeled and sliced
1 large onion, skinned and chopped
1 green pepper, seeded and chopped
2 tomatoes, skinned and chopped
1 large cooking apple, peeled and chopped
1 clove garlic, skinned and crushed
15 ml (1 tbsp) chopped fresh sage or 5 ml (1 tsp) dried sage
125 g (4 oz) lentils, cooked
15 ml (1 tbsp) raisins
30 ml (2 tbsp) unsalted peanuts
salt and freshly ground pepper
300 ml (½ pint) natural yogurt
30 g (1 oz) low-fat soft cheese

Heat the oil in a large frying pan and lightly fry the vegetables, apple, garlic and sage for 15 minutes until soft. Add the lentils raisins and peanuts. Season to taste. Stir the yogurt into the cheese and mix well. Stir into the mixture. Reheat gently for 5 minutes. Serve at once.

Putting the Eskimo Diet into Practice

We have given you a lot of information in this book. The advice on fish is simple and is the most important new message but it should be taken as a dietary package, together with our advice on saturated and unsaturated fat intake, fibre and salt. To give you a broader idea of how to bring all of this together, we have drawn up a month of sample menus which give you practical examples of how to manage healthy eating day by day.

In setting the menu, we have declared average portions but this will vary with the natural appetites and calorie needs of readers and their families. Our aim is health rather than weight reduction, although a healthy diet will naturally keep you at a healthy weight. But a hard-working labourer will need vastly more calories in his diet than a lightly-built woman working in a centrally heated office.

It will not pass your notice that we have deliberately tried to include as wide-ranging and interesting a selection of menus as possible. We also provide more than the minimum of 30 g (1 oz) a day of fatty fish and we look to the ingredients of the menu to make that low intake of less than 30 g (1 oz) per day of saturated fat as effortless as possible.

TWENTY-EIGHT DAYS OF SAMPLE MENUS

In general, we only comment on beverages, such as tea and coffee, over the first few days, so you get the idea of it. We would advise you to drink only 4 or 5 cups of normal tea or coffee per day and to make any further liquid intake either cold fruit juice or, a very palatable and acceptable alternative, a fruit squash diluted with boiling water.

Week 1

Monday

Breakfast
Porridge made with water. Sweeten with honey or a few sultanas and pour a little skimmed milk over it. A slice of wholemeal bread, toasted, with marmalade or a *light* covering of polyunsaturated margarine or low-fat spread. If it must be real butter, measure what you usually put on your knife and work out the saturated fat so that you allow it in your daily 30 g (1 oz). Try a hot orange drink instead of tea or coffee (perhaps a squash of your choice diluted with hot water).

Lunch
Tuna sandwiches, with wholemeal or another high-fibre bread, followed by fresh fruit or a low-fat yogurt. Remember that a small lunch allows you a larger family meal in the evening. If your main meal is at lunchtime, then reverse these two meals. Tea with skimmed or semi-skimmed milk. (If you want to use full-cream milk, keep to a minimum of milk and add the saturated fat content to your daily total. One full bottle of full-cream milk is more than two-thirds of your advised total daily saturated fat.)

Dinner
150 g (5 oz) grilled steak per person with mixed salad and one or two baked potatoes. Be careful with the salad cream

and dressings: choose one that is low in saturated fat, which usually tastes just as pleasant. Don't be tempted to stuff the baked potato with butter. Use low-fat cottage cheese or, better still, experiment with your own dressings using natural yogurt with mint and cucumber, which is quite delicious. Have a single glass of red wine with it.

Sweet
There is no need to deny that liking for sweet things. Try baked apple served with low-fat ice cream (see p. 159). Follow with a beverage of your choice.

Snack
What about those little food cravings late at night? Watch the calories, of course, but try a slice of wholemeal toast with low-fat smoked mackerel pâté (p. 67).

Tuesday

Breakfast
As Monday, or try the alternative – fresh grapefruit or grapefruit canned in its own juices, followed by either your favourite cereal (containing plenty of iron) and a thin slice of wholemeal toast with honey. Coffee.

Lunch
Turkey breast sandwiches with wholemeal bread. Spread the slices only very lightly with polyunsaturated margarine. This is made much easier if the margarine has been kept at room temperature long enough to soften. If you use an alternative moist filling instead of turkey, such as canned tuna or mackerel pâté, you will need no spread at all. Follow with fresh fruit or low-fat yogurt and a cup of hot fruit juice.

Dinner
Grilled trout and mashed potato. Remember to use skimmed milk with the potatoes rather than butter. Serve with lashings of soft grilled tomatoes and peas. Optional – one small glass of white wine.

Sweet
Meringue nest with fresh fruit, topped with low-fat fruit yogurt or fromage frais. Beverage of your choice.

Snack
For a night-time (or elevenses) snack, try 2 Ryvita with cottage cheese, topped with a quartered tomato and a couple of slices of cucumber, seasoned with freshly ground pepper. Avoid tea or coffee late at night because of the caffeine content. Try squash with boiling water instead.

Wednesday

Breakfast
Fruit juice followed by two Weetabix, sweetened with sultanas and hot skimmed milk poured over. Tea.

Lunch
Stir-fried herrings and vegetables (see p. 77) served with wholemeal bread. Follow with a cup of coffee (not necessary to take decaffeinated if you do not drink more than 4 or 5 cups of tea or coffee in a day). One pear.

Dinner
Chicken with mustard sauce (see p. 154) served with new or boiled potatoes and vegetables such as broccoli and carrots.

Sweet
Fresh pineapple or canned pineapple in its own juice.

Snack
Breakfast cereal (half portion), with hot or cold skimmed milk. Hot fruit juice.

Thursday

Breakfast
Kippers with a slice of wholemeal toast, followed by a refreshing glass of chilled fresh fruit juice. Note that frozen packaged kippers often arrive with butter in the bag. Either buy your kippers fresh or remove from the pack, take out

the butter, and then grill. Follow with a cup of tea with skimmed milk. For somebody who is used to full-cream milk in their tea, this will take some getting used to and perhaps it might be easier to evolve through semi-skimmed or even to keep to semi-skimmed in tea. But taking larger quantities of milk introduces a real possibility of quite a lot of saturated fat – see comparison table of different types of milk on page 46.

Lunch
Baked beans on toast. Followed with mixed fruit salad, topped, if liked, with low-fat natural yogurt. Tea.

Dinner
Vegetable curry (see p. 169).

Sweet
Fruit jelly with real fruit, such as unsweetened pears or peaches and natural yogurt topping. (Ice cream would also go with jelly or fruit salads and low-fat ice cream is available.)

Snack
Slice of hot wholemeal toast with your favourite jam, or two low-fat biscuits.

Friday

Breakfast
Fresh unsweetened fruit juice. A boiled or poached egg with wholemeal toast.

Lunch
Cold roast chicken or turkey breast with potatoes, salad and wholemeal bread.

Dinner
Mackerel with orange sauce (see p. 97). Serve with boiled potatoes and vegetables. One of the best ways of cooking vegetables is in the pressure cooker or the microwave. Aim to get your moisture with the meal from the vegetables rather than from a buttery or creamy sauce.

Sweet
Stewed apple (or fruit of your choice) with a small portion
of low-fat ice cream.

Snack
Banana.

Saturday

Breakfast
Cereal with skimmed milk and sultanas. Slice of wholemeal
toast with honey or marmalade.

Lunch
Lean ham sandwiches with mustard – or even better still if
your purse or pocket will run to it, smoked salmon or
smoked trout sandwiches – and side salad or low-calorie
coleslaw.

Dinner
Paupiettes of plaice (see p. 109), or as an alternative
microwave meal, Tangy cod steaks (see p. 118).

Sweet
Raspberry surprise (see p. 160).

Snack
A couple of morning coffee biscuits.

Sunday

Breakfast
If the dinner is to be a red meat roast, then why not start the
day with grilled kippers, which will counter the blood fat
effects of the main meal. Put the kippers directly on to dry
wholemeal toast – the oil in the kippers is moist enough to
make up for any butter or even margarine.

Lunch
Crab and corn soup (see p. 69) with granary rolls. Followed
with half a 425 g (15 oz) can low-fat rice pudding. Instead of
jam, put a few strawberry halves in the middle.

Dinner
Roast beef (see p. 148). Serve with baked potatoes and two vegetables, steamed in the pressure cooker or cooked in the microwave. If you like to use a gravy, choose a mix such as Bisto, which does not have added fat. Bisto contains its own salt so you do not need to add any to the cooking.

Sweet
Treat yourself to home-baked apple pie, but try to cut back on the pastry and be sure to use only polyunsaturated margarine. Allow yourself a little single cream on this one day; alternatively low-fat ice cream or natural yogurt.

Snack
If turkey or salmon was the main meal, a little of this in a wholemeal sandwich.

Week 2

Monday

Breakfast
Half a grapefruit, grilled. Follow with 2 Weetabix, sprinkled with a few sultanas with hot skimmed milk. Tea or coffee.

Lunch
Tuna and salad sandwiches. Use one small can of tuna and plenty of salad on wholemeal or granary bread. Fruit yogurt or fresh fruit.

Dinner
Turkey fillets with mushrooms (see p. 152) served with potatoes, broccoli and carrots.

Sweet
Fresh fruit salad topped with a little low-fat fruit yogurt.

Snack
Toast and honey.

Tuesday

Breakfast
A glass of unsweetened orange followed by 2 shredded wheat with hot milk. Tea or coffee.

Lunch
One slice of ham and mushroom pizza with salad, followed by fresh pear. Tea or coffee.

Dinner
Grilled mackerel with sage sauce (see p. 91) served with plenty of vegetables, boiled potatoes or rice.
For an alternative microwave meal, try Fruity stuffed mackerel (see p. 125).

Sweet
Peaches and low-calorie fruit yogurt.

Snack
Two biscuits and decaffeinated coffee (caffeine tends to keep you awake at night).

Wednesday

Breakfast
A glass of unsweetened grapefruit juice followed by poached or scrambled egg on wholemeal toast. Tea or coffee.

Lunch
Chicken and cheese salad (see p. 159), followed by a slice of melon.

Dinner
Shepherd's pie (see general tips on cutting down fat in cooking, p. 51), served with carrots and green beans.

Sweet
Slimline orange sorbet (see p. 161).

Snack
Fromage frais with tea or fruit drink.

Thursday

Breakfast
Porridge made with water and topped with a little skimmed milk and 5 ml (1 tsp) honey. Tea or coffee.

Lunch
Prawns with salad of your choice and a slice of wholemeal bread or a small roll, followed by low-fat fromage frais.

Dinner
Salmon steaks with cucumber sauce (see p. 128).

Sweet
Stewed rhubarb topped with low-fat yogurt.

Snack
Fresh fruit.

Friday

Breakfast
A glass of unsweetened orange juice. Grilled or poached kippers with 1 slice of wholemeal bread. Tea or coffee.

Lunch
Crispbreads with low-fat cottage cheese (with chives or pineapple if preferred). A slice of Mixed fruit teabread (see p. 163).

Dinner
Chicken Véronique (see p. 149) served with vegetables.

Sweet
Meringue nest filled with strawberries or raspberries and topped with a litte low-fat fruit yogurt. A glass of white wine (optional).

Snack
Half portion of breakfast cereal of choice.

Saturday

Breakfast
Bran flakes with sultanas and skimmed milk. Unsweetened fruit juice or a piece of fresh fruit. Tea or coffee.

Lunch
Pasta with hot tuna sauce (see p. 85). Pineapple chunks canned with own juice.

Dinner
175 g (6 oz) grilled pork fillet with salad and baked potatoes.

Sweet
Strawberries topped with a little ice cream.

Snack
Small portion of rice pudding with jam.

Sunday

Breakfast
Wholemeal toast with honey or marmalade followed by fresh fruit. Tea or coffee.

Lunch
Roast turkey with a selection of vegetables and boiled new potatoes. (Remember to skim off the fat from the turkey stock before making gravy.) Follow with a portion of apple or rhubarb crumble (topping made with polyunsaturated margarine) with a little custard made with skimmed milk.

Dinner
Cold turkey sandwich or salad. A slice of Mixed fruit teabread (see p. 163).

Snack
A thin slice of wholemeal bread with sandwich filling of your choice, possibly banana.

Week 3

Monday

Breakfast
Weetabix with sultanas and hot skimmed milk. A slice of wholemeal toast with hot orange drink.

Lunch
Crisp and crunchy plaice salad (see p. 85) with a wholemeal roll. Fresh or defrosted raspberries with low-fat ice cream.

Dinner
Red kidney bean hot-pot (see p. 168).

Sweet
Portion of Slimline orange sorbet (see p. 161). (Remember, cholesterol is in egg yolk only.)

Snack
Toasted teacake with a little jam.

Tuesday

Breakfast
Bran flakes with skimmed milk. Two slices of pineapple canned in juice. Tea or coffee.

Lunch
Thick bean and vegetable soup (see p. 166) with hot crusty roll. Low-fat fruit yogurt. Hot orange drink.

Dinner
Savoury halibut (see p. 107).

Sweet
Fresh fruit salad with 15 ml (1 tbsp) single cream or Shape.

Snack
Slice of Mixed fruit teabread (see p. 163).

Wednesday

Breakfast
Porridge made with water and sweetened with honey or sultanas. Hot orange drink.

Lunch
Sardines on two slices of wholemeal toast. Follow with Baked apple (see p. 159). Tea or coffee.

Dinner
Grilled red meat of your choice with boiled or baked potatoes and vegetables of your choice.

Sweet
Banana split made with low-fat ice cream and fresh strawberries or raspberries.

Snack
Kipper pâté (see p. 66) on crispbread.

Thursday

Breakfast
Kippers on hot wholemeal toast, followed by refreshing cold fruit drink. Tea or decaffeinated coffee.

Lunch
Low-fat cheese salad (such as Edam low-fat) and French bread. Rice pudding made with semi-skimmed milk and topped with raspberries.

Dinner
Wholewheat pasta with ratatouille sauce (see p.170).

Sweet
Raspberry surprise (see p. 160).

Snack
Fresh fruit of your choice.

Friday

Breakfast
Fruit juice. Two Weetabix sweetened with sultanas with hot skimmed milk. Tea or decaffeinated coffee.

Lunch
Moules à la marinière (see p. 80) with hot French bread. Low-fat yogurt or fresh fruit. Hot orange drink.

Dinner
Turkey fillets with mushrooms (see p. 152).

Sweet
Small portion of hot fruit pie with low-fat ice cream, or low-fat fromage frais.

Snack
Crispbread with cottage cheese.

Saturday

Breakfast
Muesli with skimmed milk. Two thin slices of toast with honey. Tea.

Lunch
Slices of lean ham with a mixed salad and a little low-fat coleslaw. Serve with hot crusty French bread. Follow with fruit yogurt and a decaffeinated coffee.

Dinner
Paupiettes of sole with salmon mousseline (see p.140). As an alternative microwave meal, try Paper-wrapped lemon fillet (see p. 122).

Sweet
Slice of apple pie or crumble with low-fat ice cream.

Snack
Crispbread with smoked mackerel pâté (see p. 67).

Sunday

Breakfast
Half a grapefruit, grilled, with a pinch of brown sugar.
Wholemeal toast and honey.

Lunch
Scrambled or poached egg on toast, followed by fresh fruit.

Dinner
Argyll salmon with oranges and pasta (see p. 101).

Sweet
Peach pavlova (see p. 160). (Remember the yolk contains
the cholesterol.)

Tea
Lean meat sandwiches of your choice. Fresh fruit salad.

Snack
Two Rich Tea biscuits.

Week 4

Monday

Breakfast
Bran flakes with skimmed milk. Unsweetened orange or
grapefruit juice.

Lunch
Tuna salad with French bread, or tuna and cucumber
sandwiches. Fruit of choice.

Dinner
Vegetarian medley (see p. 171). Notice that the usual butter
is replaced by olive oil. Choose a low-fat cheese from the list
on p. 47). For dessert, serve meringue nests with fruit and
low-fat fromage frais.

Snack
Kipper or mackerel pâté on a thin slice of toast.

Tuesday

Breakfast
Two Weetabix with skimmed milk and sultanas. Unsweetened fruit juice. Tea or coffee.

Lunch
Tomato herrings with warm pitta bread (see p. 78). Apple or fruit of your choice; as an alternative microwave meal, try Herring salad (see p. 121).

Dinner
Chicken in a pot (see p.156).

Sweet
Oaty bar (see p.165).

Snack
Low-fat fromage frais.

Wednesday

Breakfast
Toasted wholemeal muffin with honey or marmalade. Unsweetened fruit juice. Tea or coffee.

Lunch
Salad sandwiches using lots of lettuce, cucumber, tomato, spring onion, beetroot and cress with a little low-calorie salad cream to moisten. Fresh fruit, low-fat yogurt or an Oaty bar (see p. 165).

Dinner
Why not lighten your midweek with Stuffed sea bass braised in white wine (see p. 134).
Serve with new potatoes or rice, with mange tout or sweetcorn.

Sweet
Grape poached pears (see p. 161).

Snack
Two Rich Tea fingers.

Thursday

Breakfast
Bran flakes with skimmed milk. Two slices of pineapple canned in its own juice. Tea or coffee.

Lunch
Baked potato topped with low-fat cottage cheese and chives with a mixed salad. Slice of melon or an orange.

Dinner
Baked gingered chicken (see p. 151) served with boiled potatoes and ratatouille.

Sweet
Pineapple dessert (see p. 162).

Snack
A handful of raisins with unsalted peanuts.

Friday

Breakfast
Choose any breakfast from the week. Hot fruit drink.

Lunch
Minestrone soup (see p. 166) with a hot crusty roll. Slice of Mixed fruit teabread (see p. 163). Tea.

Dinner
Salmon and prawn tagliatelle (see p. 91) served with a side salad.

Sweet
Spiced pears (see p. 163).

Snack
Fresh fruit. Drink of your choice.

Saturday

Breakfast
Bran flakes with banana slices and raisins. Thin slice of toast and honey. Decaffeinated coffee.

Lunch
Mackerel and potato salad with white bread and polyunsaturated margarine.

Dinner
Self-indulgence day with grilled 225 g (8 oz) beef steak per portion, served with a choice of baked or roast potatoes (roast in vegetable oil) and salad or two vegetables of your choice.

Sweet
A slice of French apple and ginger cake (see p. 164).

Snack
Just a cup of tea.

Sunday

Breakfast
Boiled or poached egg and toast. Hot grilled grapefruit with a little brown sugar.

Dinner
Lobster Newburg (see p. 137) with a glass of Vinho Verde, served with boiled rice and a colourful and varied side salad.

Sweet
Flamed Jamaican bananas (see p. 162).

Snack
A piece of fresh fruit and a cup of tea.

Final Word of Advice

We realize that changes in your diet, or in your family's eating habits, will only come about by a slow process of trying and testing. The harassed shopper or cook will only have a short time available for thinking about fat contents and will, in real life, tend to evolve a natural balance, based on past experience and personal taste. We have tried to give examples that will enable you to work towards the fat intakes we recommend. The last thing we really want is to convert people from a cholesterol hypochondriasis to a saturated fat and fish hypochondriasis. You will not go far wrong if you couple understanding with a sense of humour in all this and if you allow your natural common sense and balance to prevail.

Good health and happy eating.

Dr Reg Saynor and Dr Frank Ryan

Index